Powder Room

a sumo studios publication

PHOTOGRAPHER: PAUL MALHERBE
MODEL: SASHI

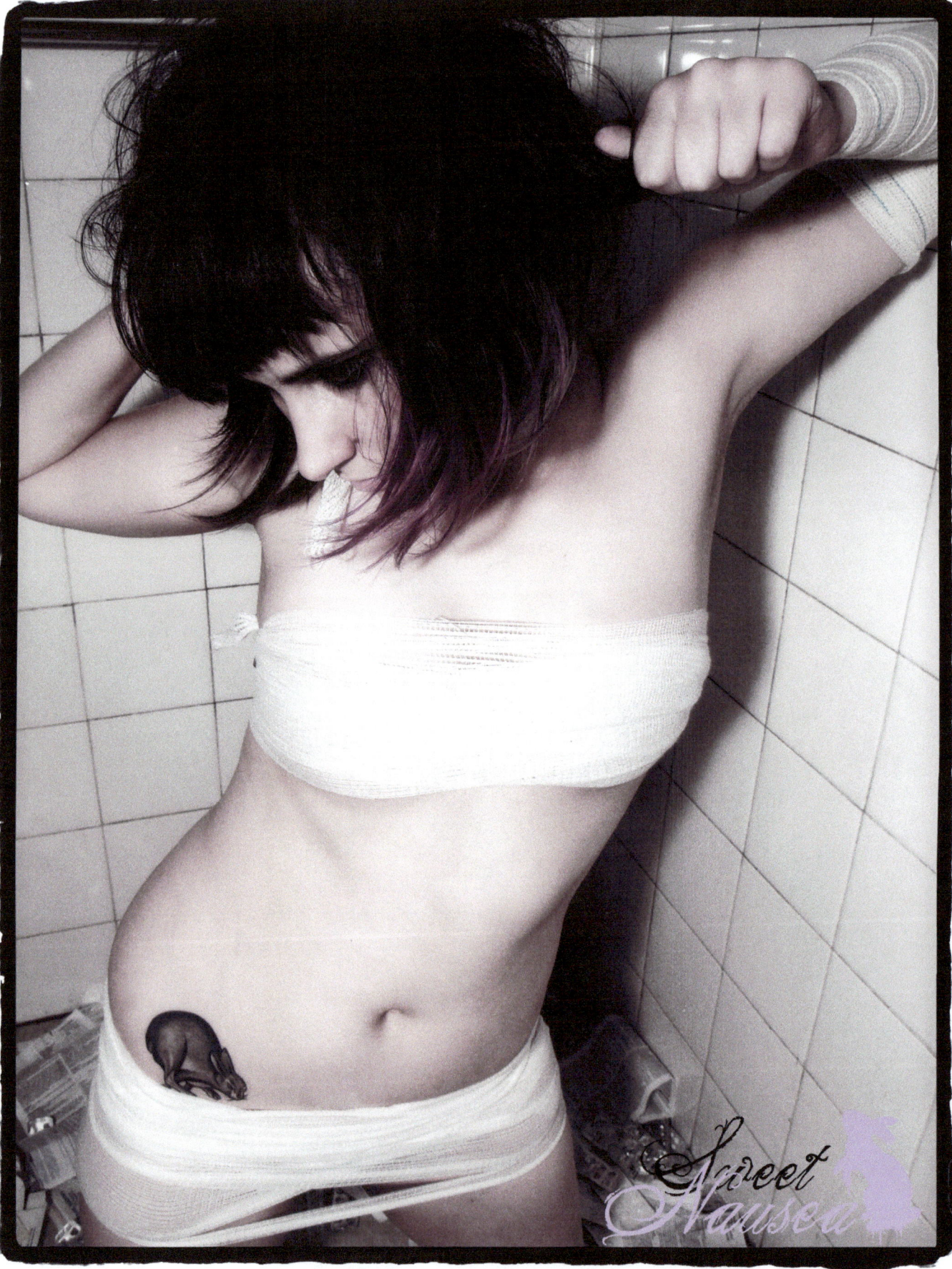

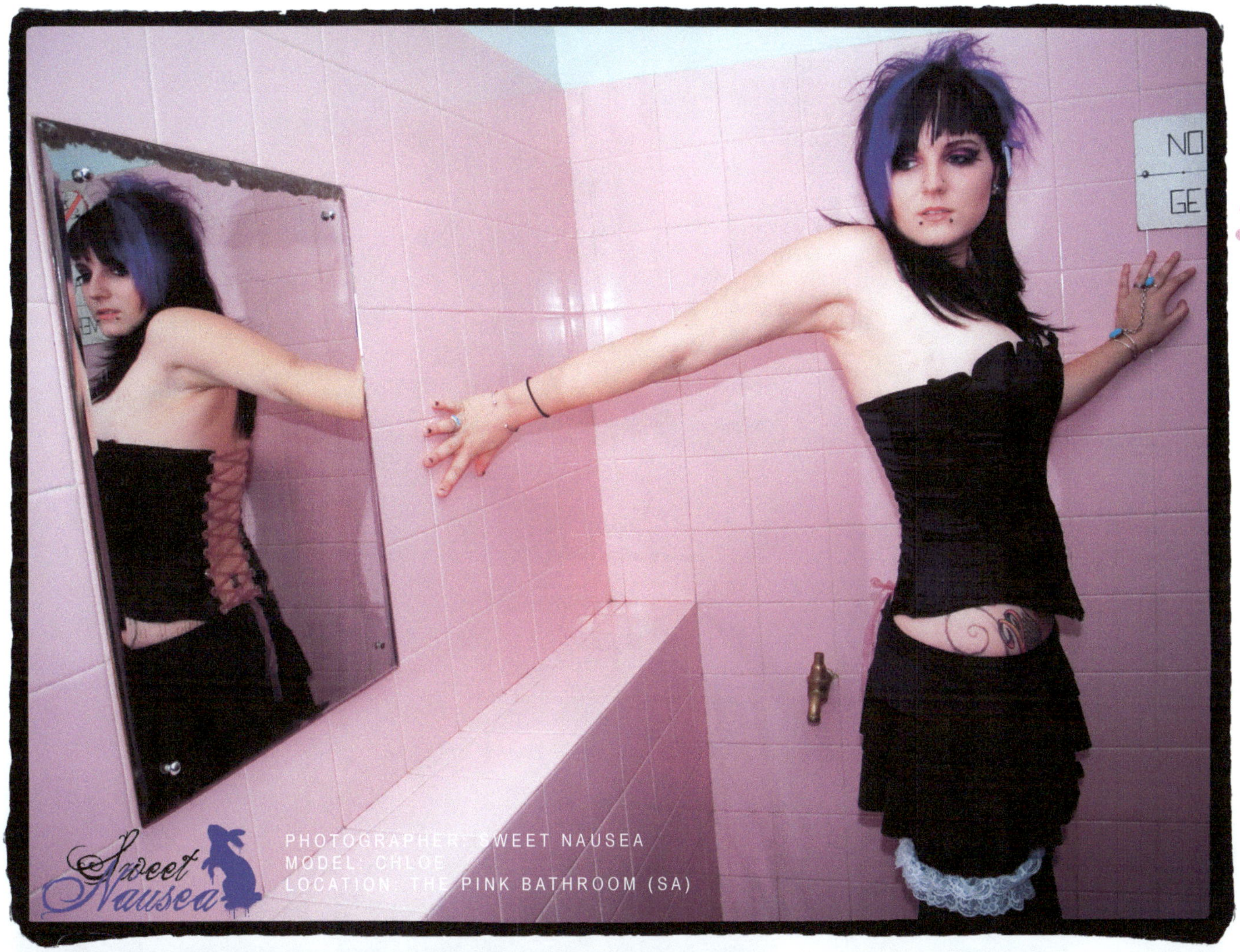

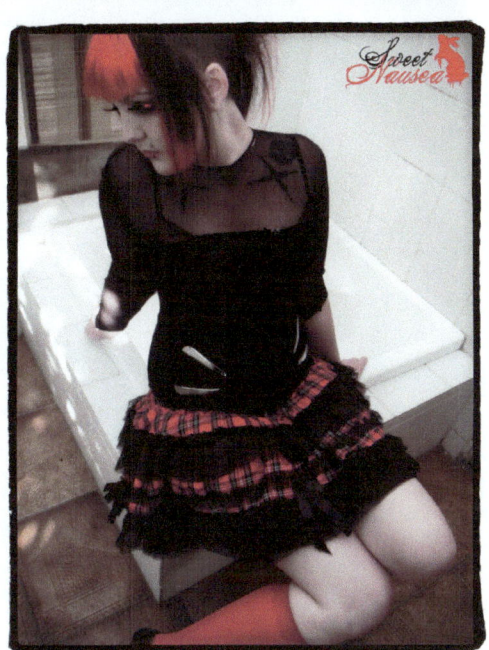

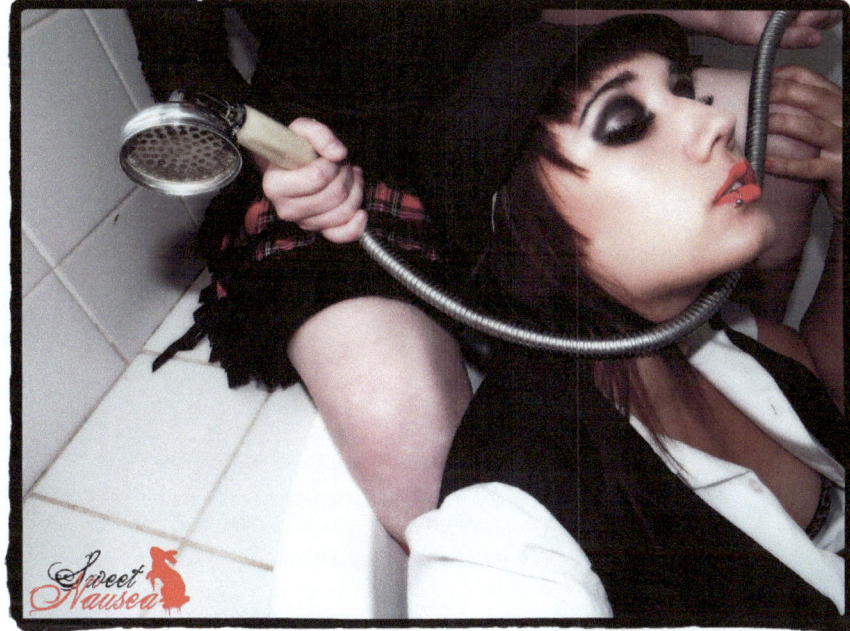

PHOTOGRAPHER: SWEET NAUSEA
MODEL: CHLOE
LOCATION: THE PINK BATHROOM (SA)

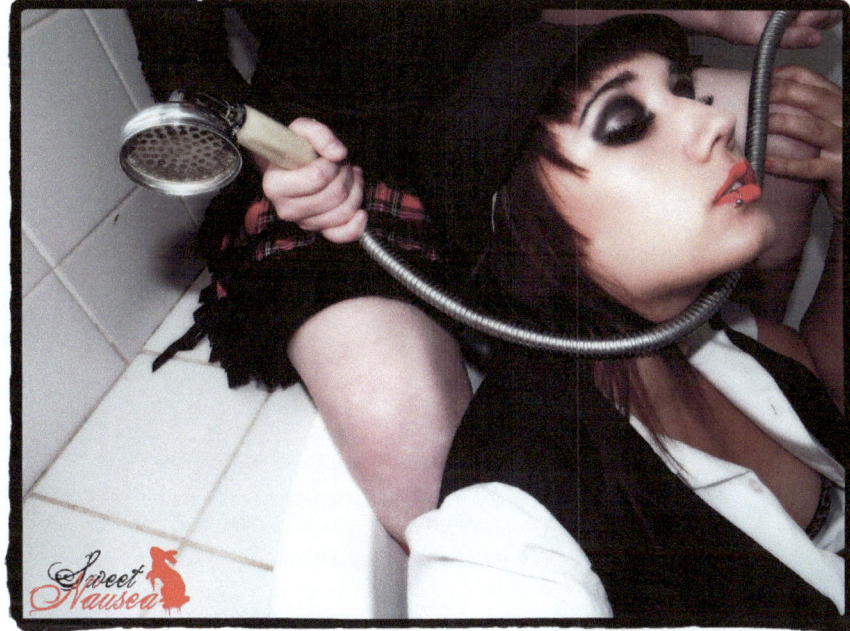

PHOTOGRAPHER: SWEET NAUSEA
MODEL: MAX
LOCATION: UNKNOWN (SA)

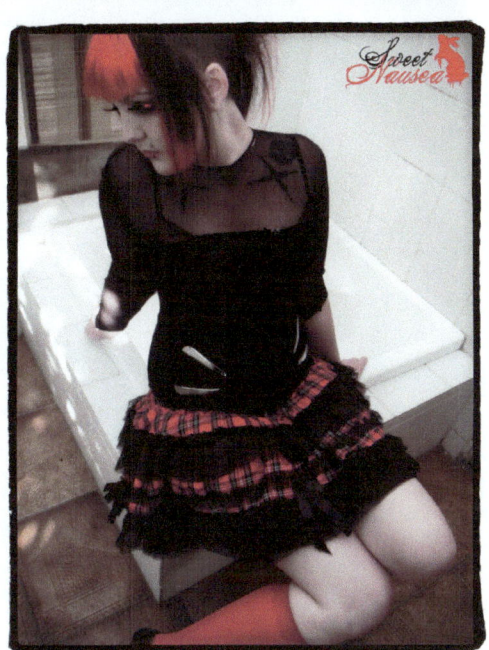

PHOTOGRAPHER: SWEET NAUSEA
MODEL: LISA
LOCATION: UNKNOWN (SA)

4

PHOTOGRAPHER: BEDLAM PHOTOGRAPHY
MODEL: DOLLIE
LOCATION: BEDLAM BATHROOM (US)

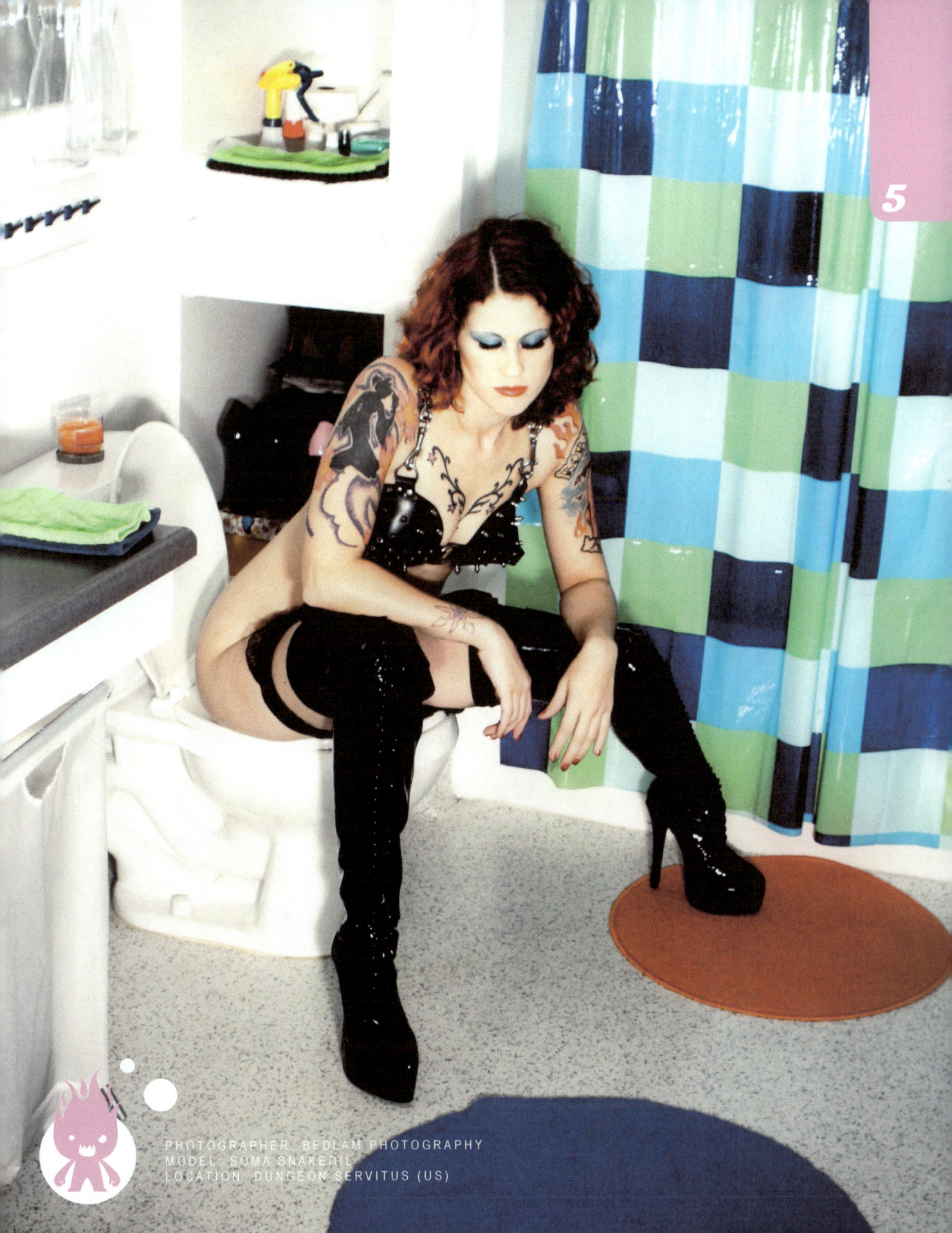

PHOTOGRAPHER BEDLAM PHOTOGRAPHY
MODEL SOMA SNAKEOIL
LOCATION DUNGEON SERVITUS (US)

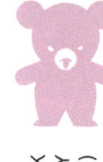

PHOTOGRAPHER: BRENDAN JACK AKA DR. JACK
MODEL: ALLY
LOCATION: ALLY'S BATHROOM (SA)

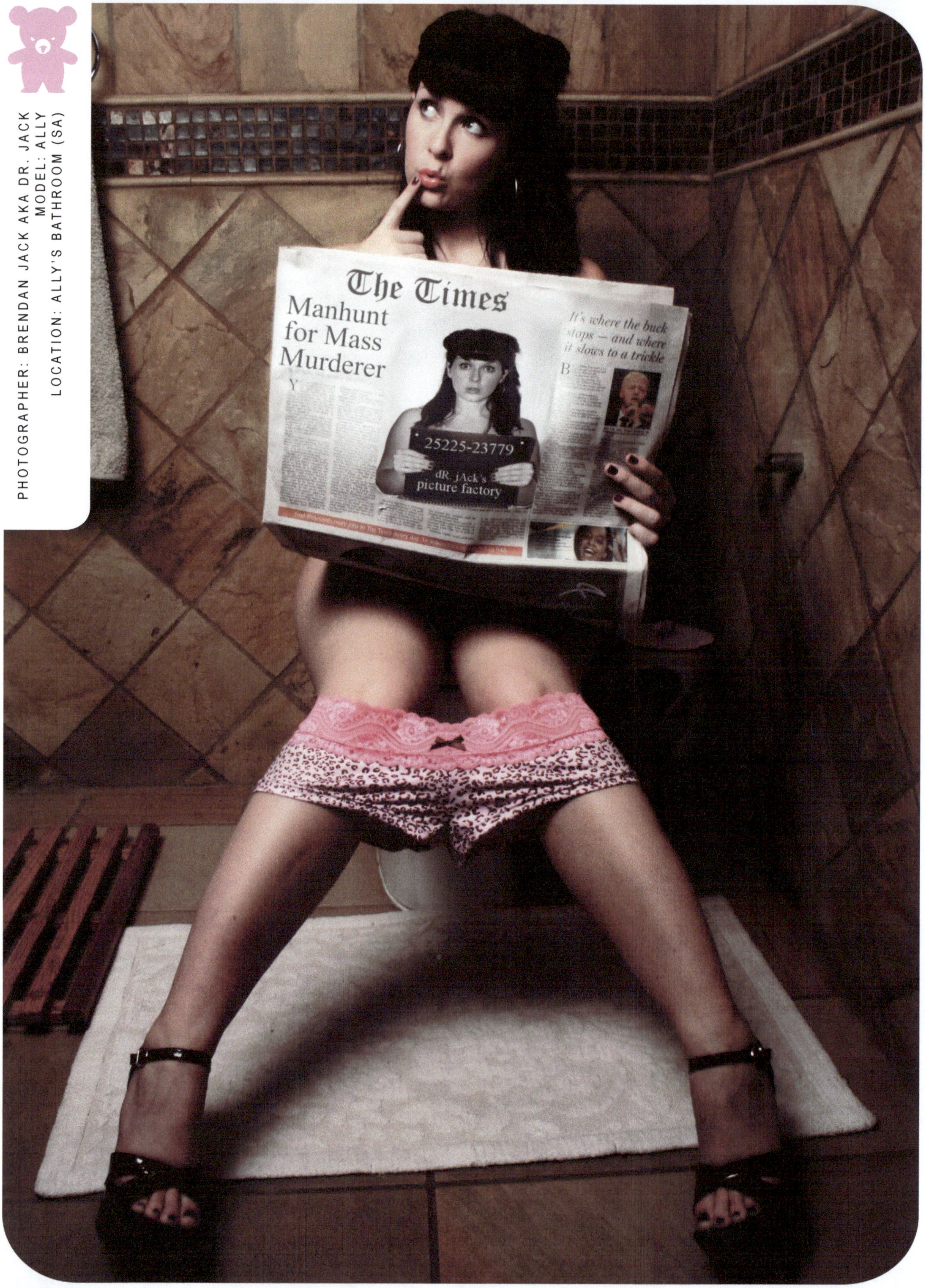

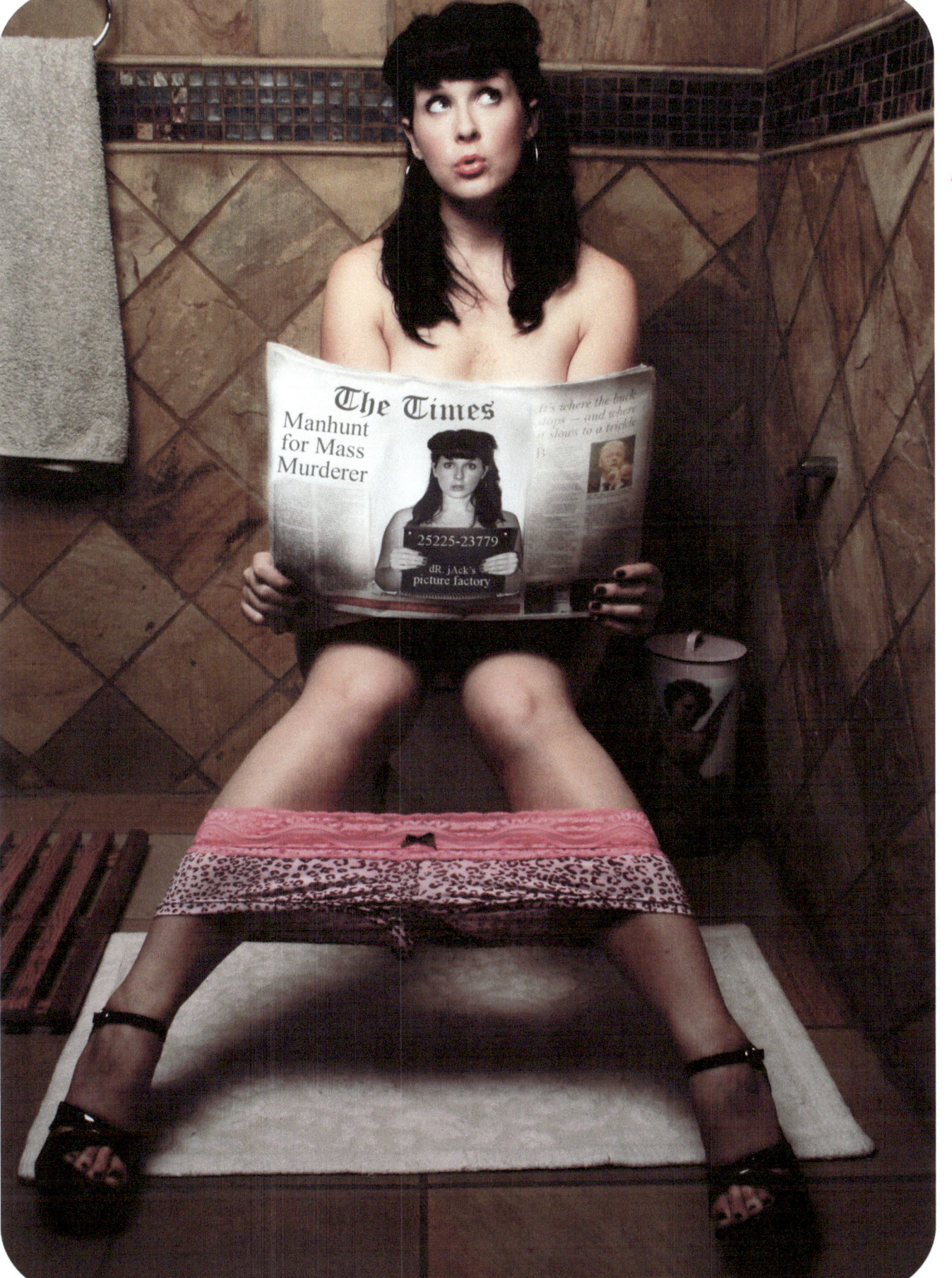

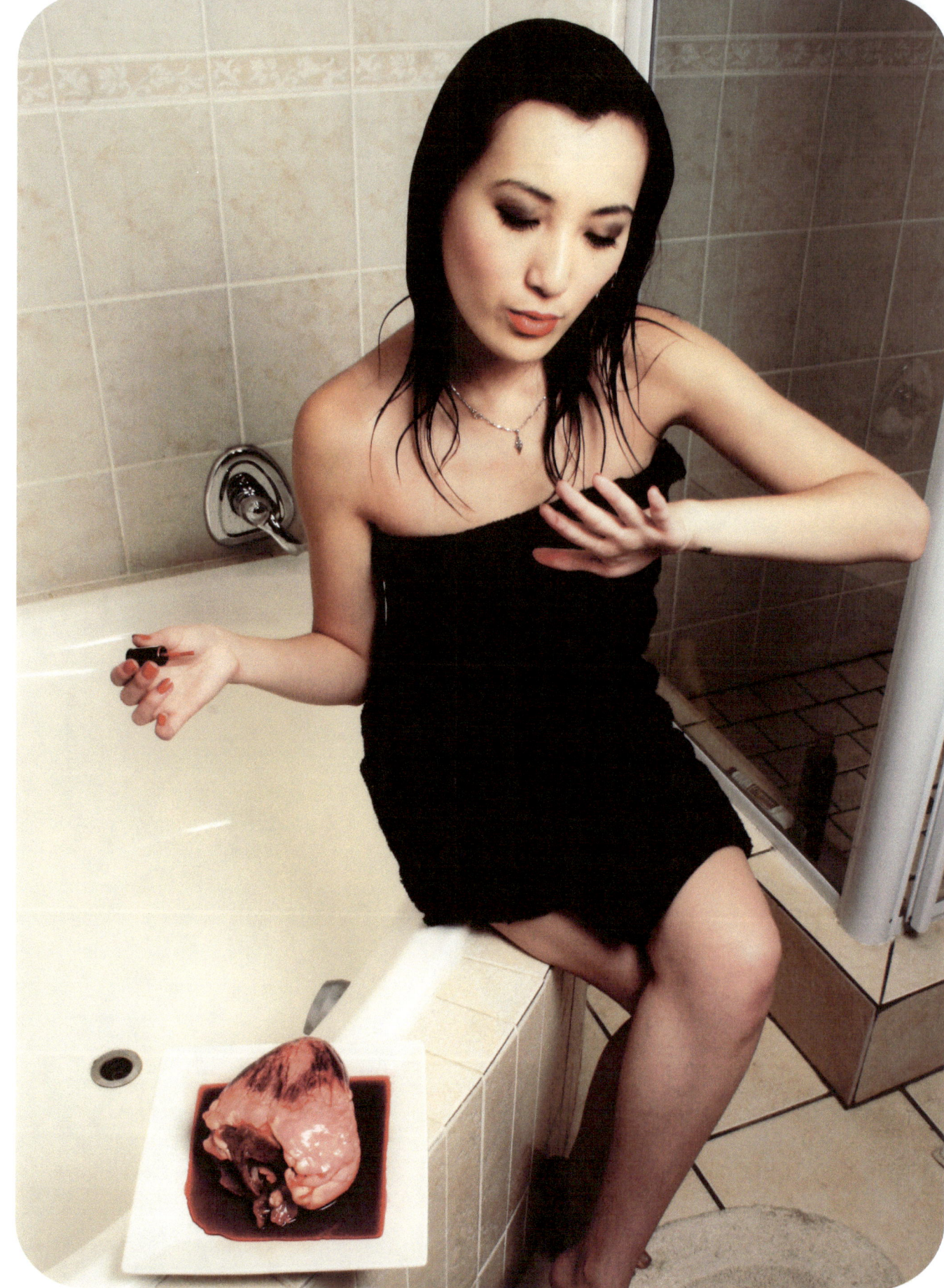

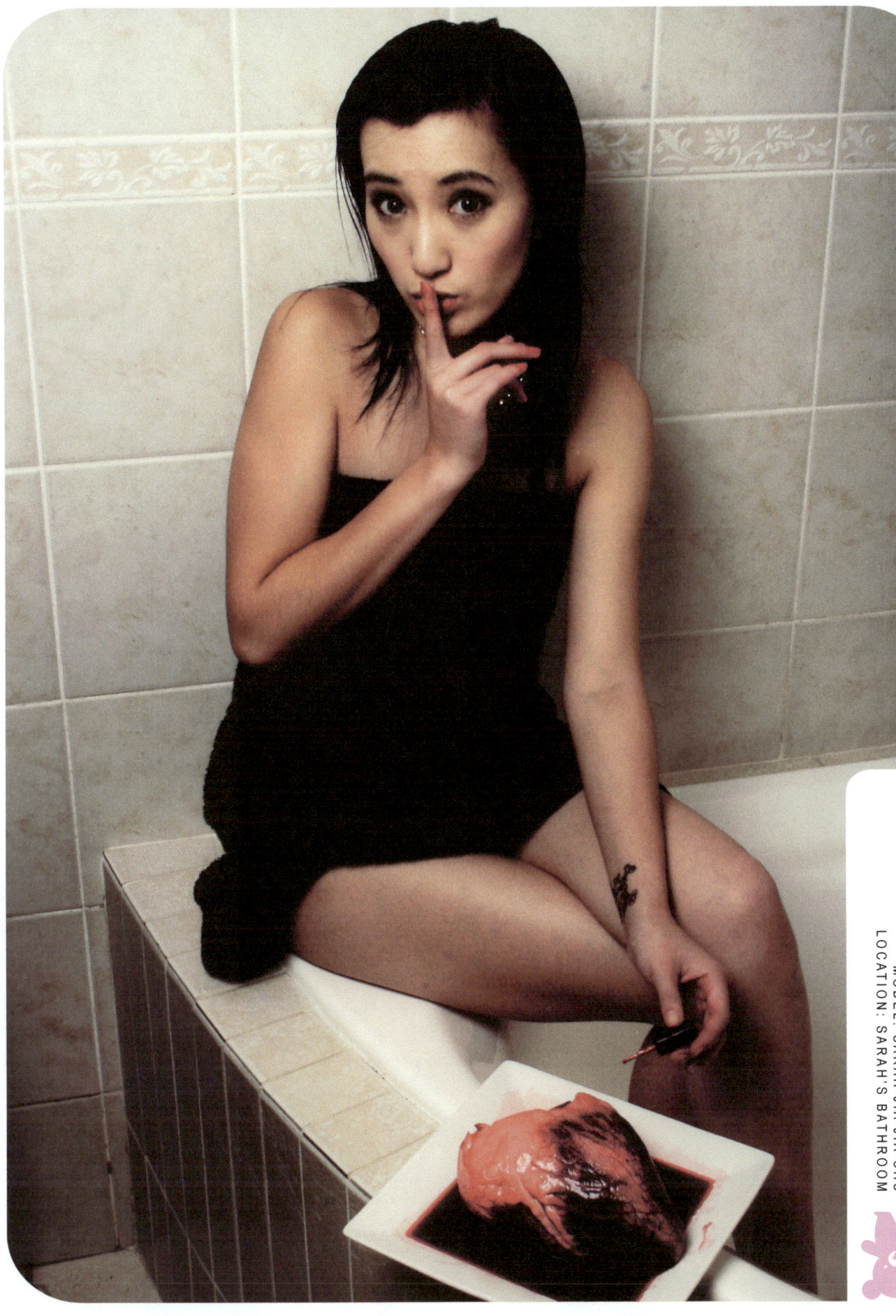

PHOTOGRAPHER: BRENDAN JACK AKA DR. JACK
MODEL: SARAH JIA JIA CHU
LOCATION: SARAH'S BATHROOM

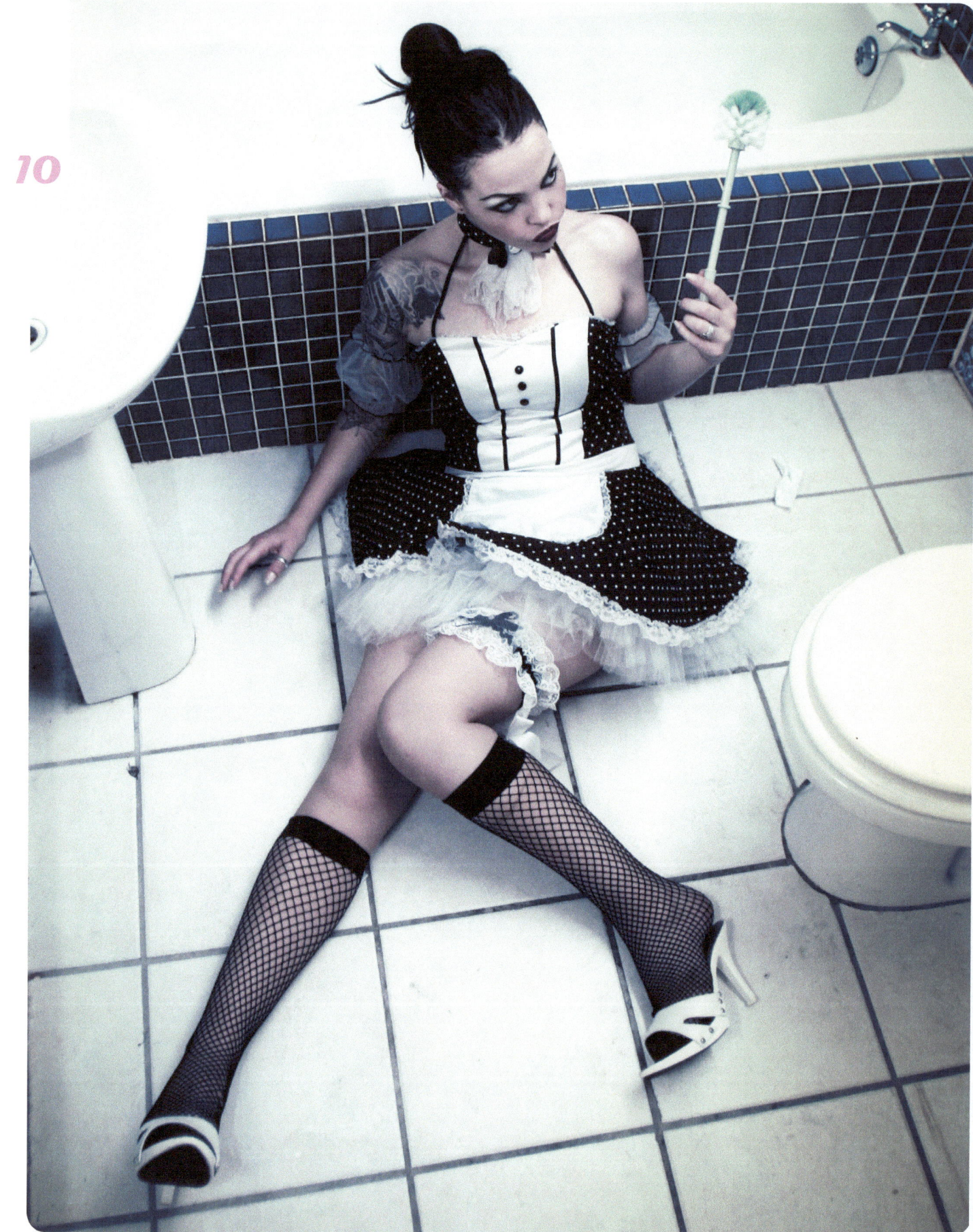

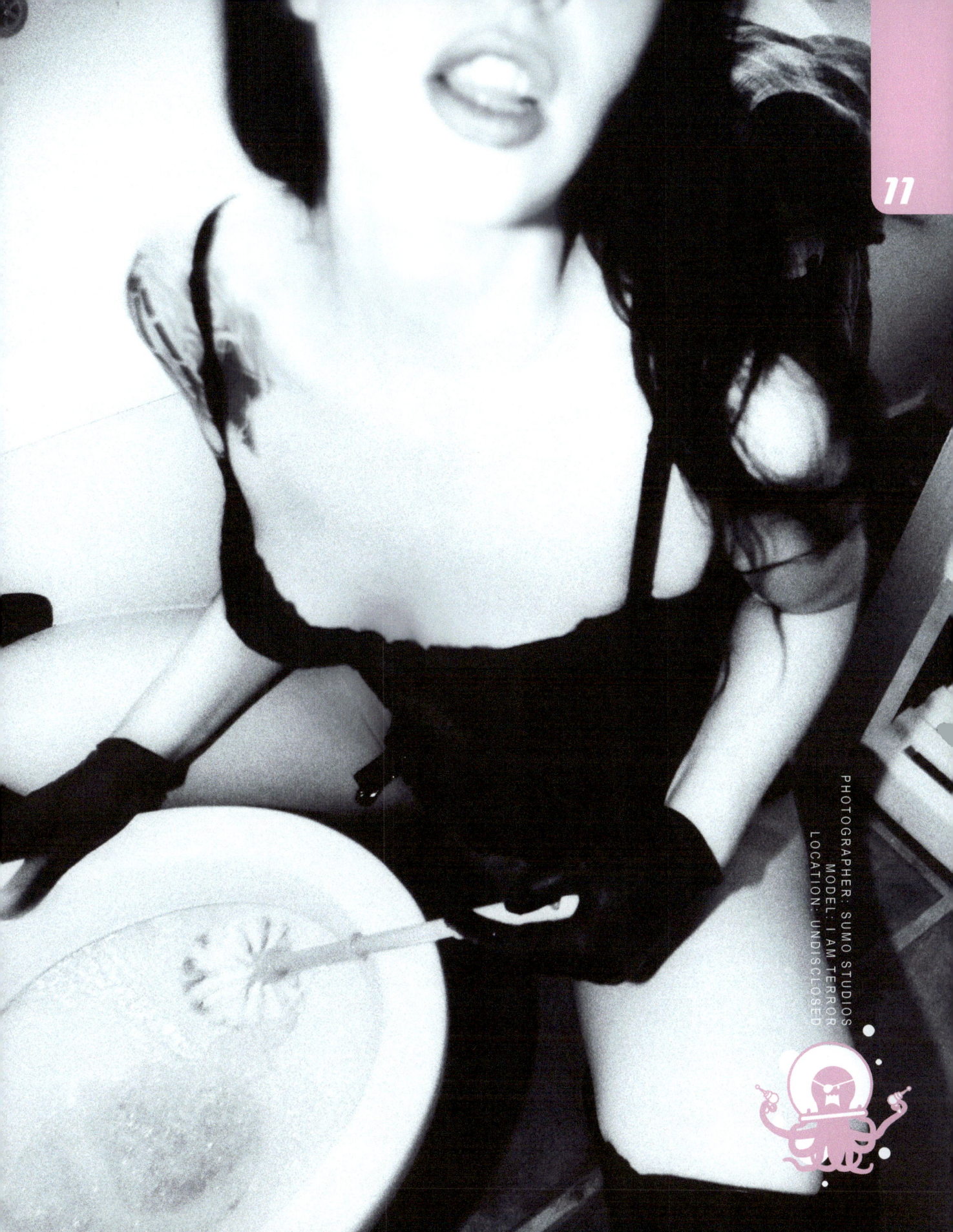

PHOTOGRAPHER: SUMO STUDIOS
MODEL: I AM TERROR
LOCATION: UNDISCLOSED

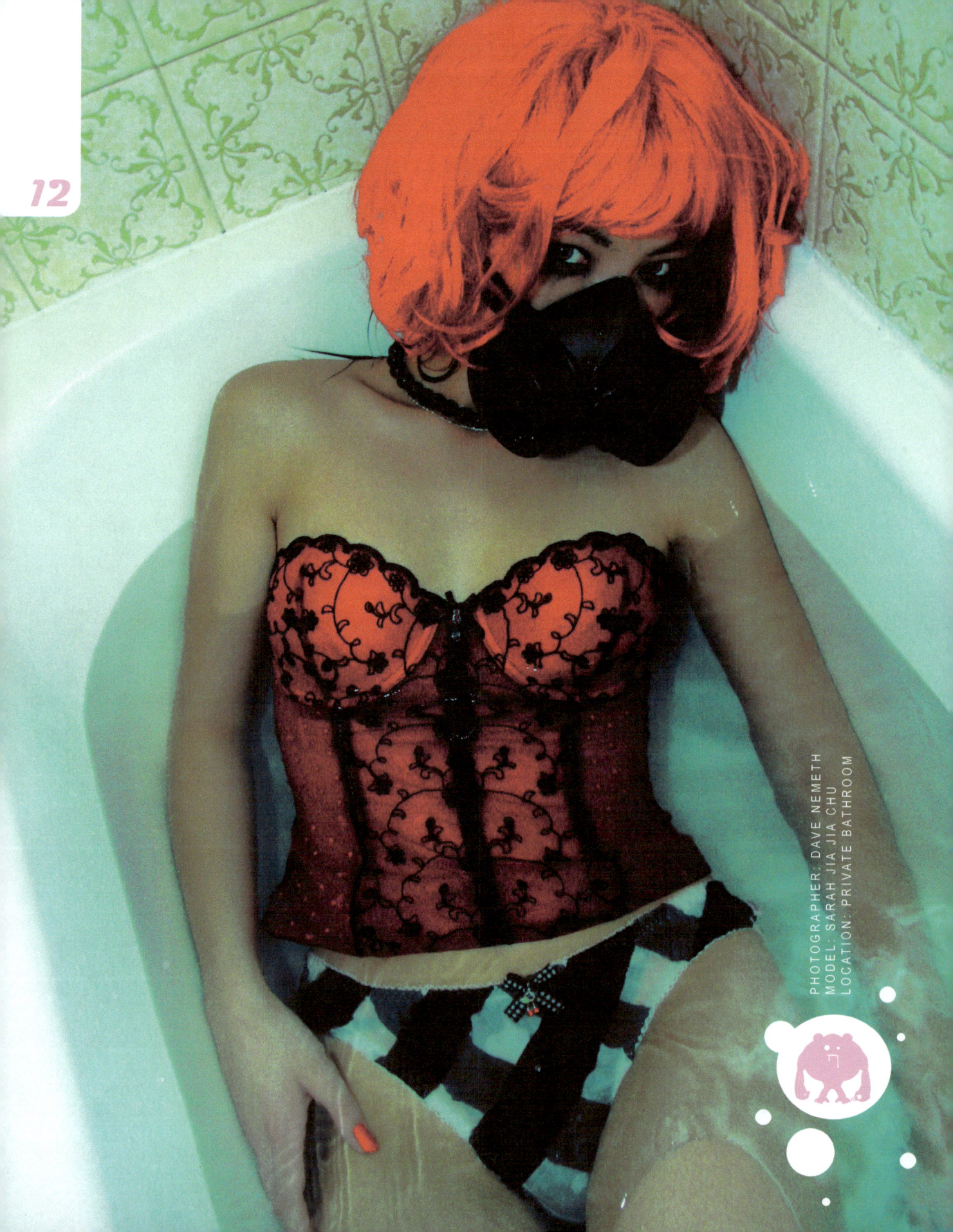

PHOTOGRAPHER: DAVE NEMETH
MODEL: SARAH JIA JIA CHU
LOCATION: PRIVATE BATHROOM

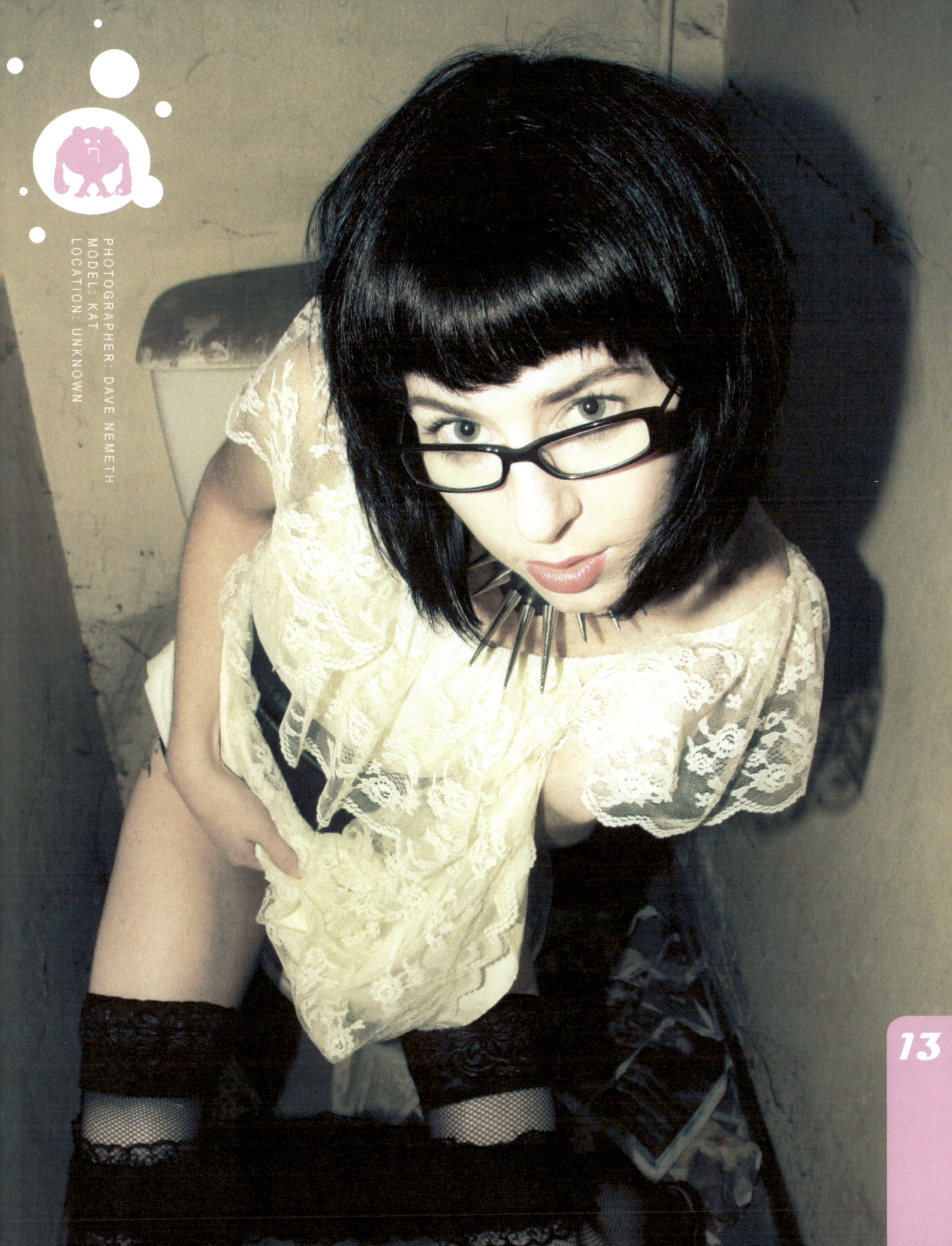

PHOTOGRAPHER: DAVE NEMETH
MODEL: KAT
LOCATION: UNKNOWN

13

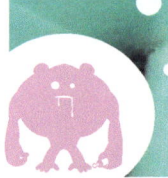

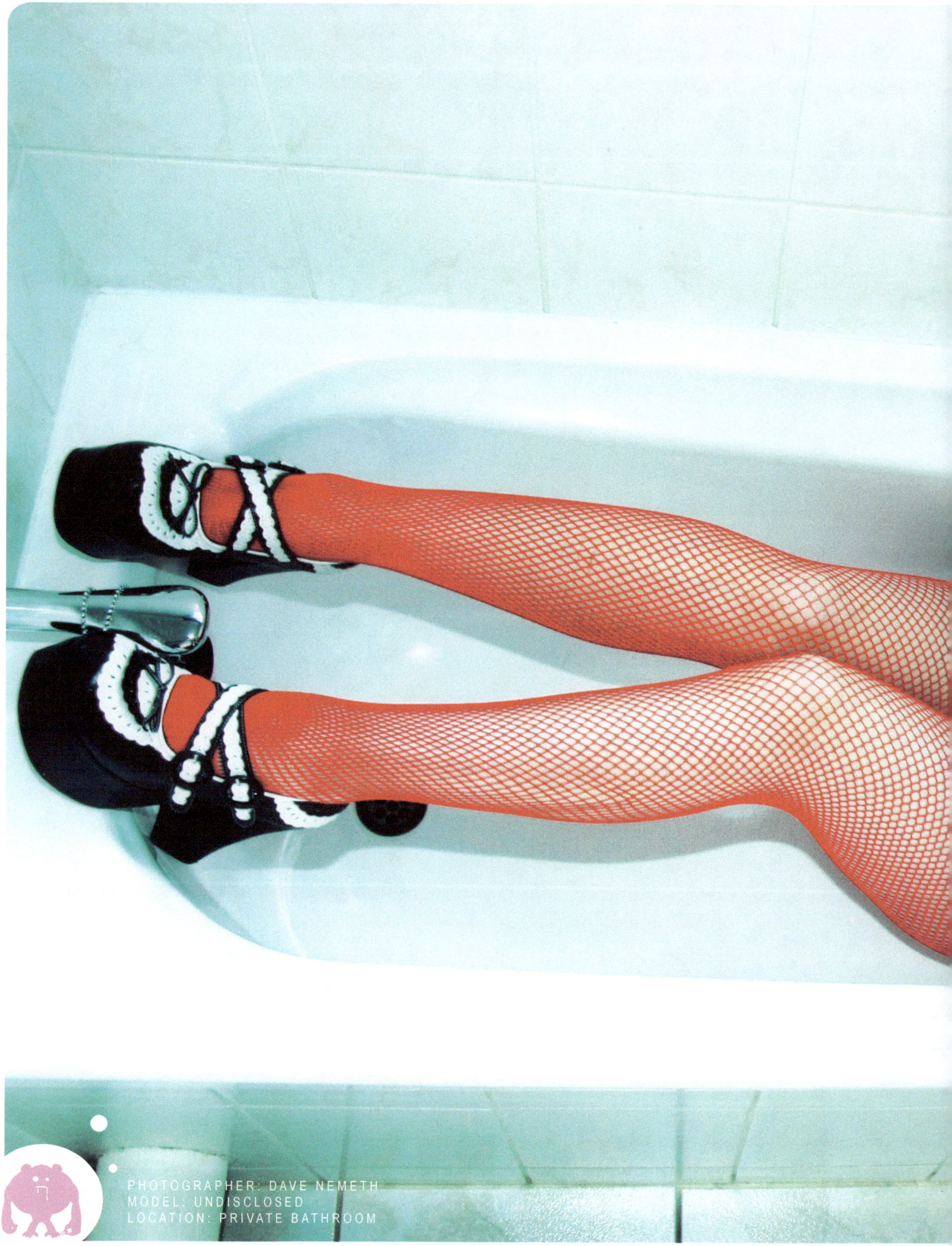

PHOTOGRAPHER: DAVE NEMETH
MODEL: UNDISCLOSED
LOCATION: PRIVATE BATHROOM

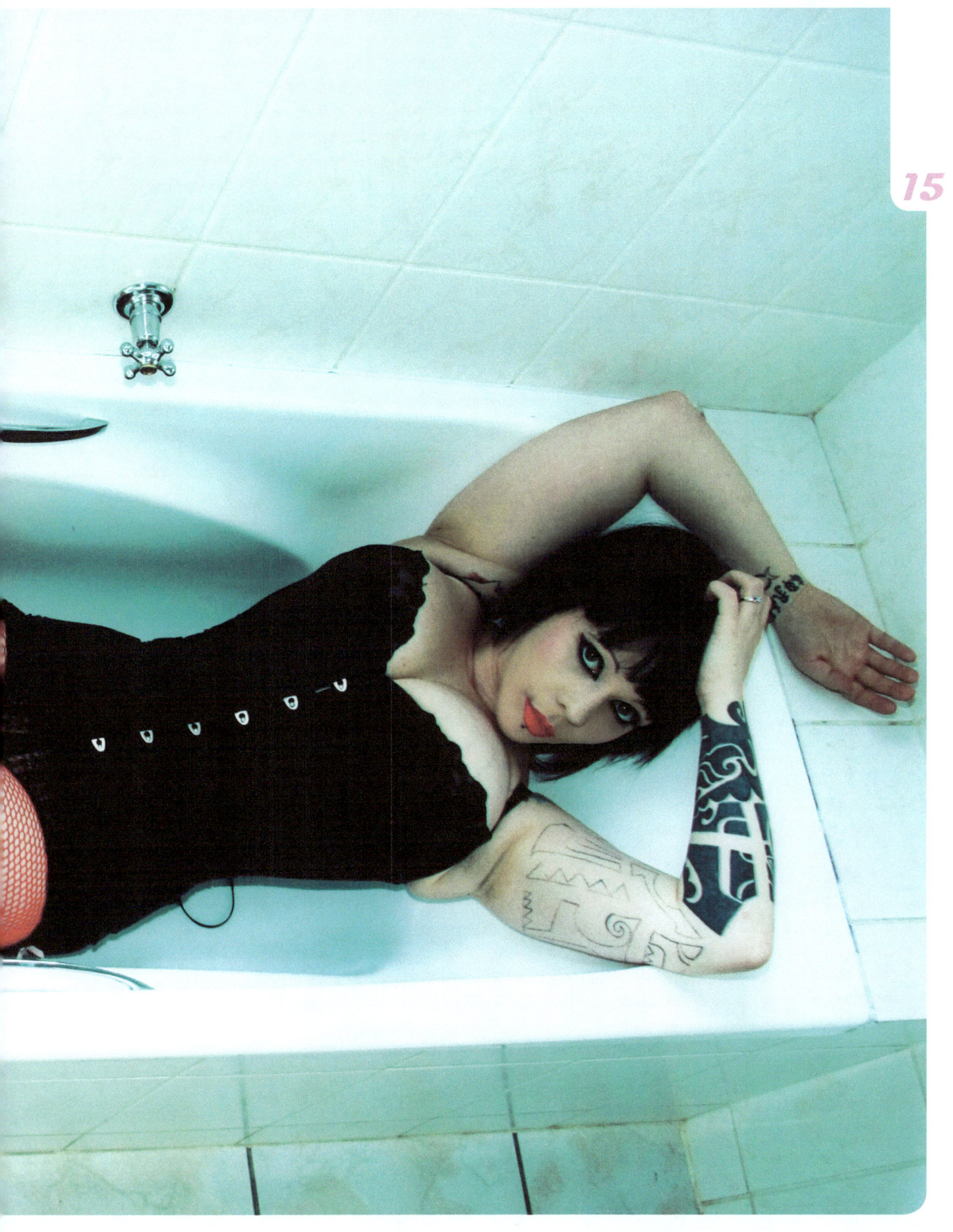

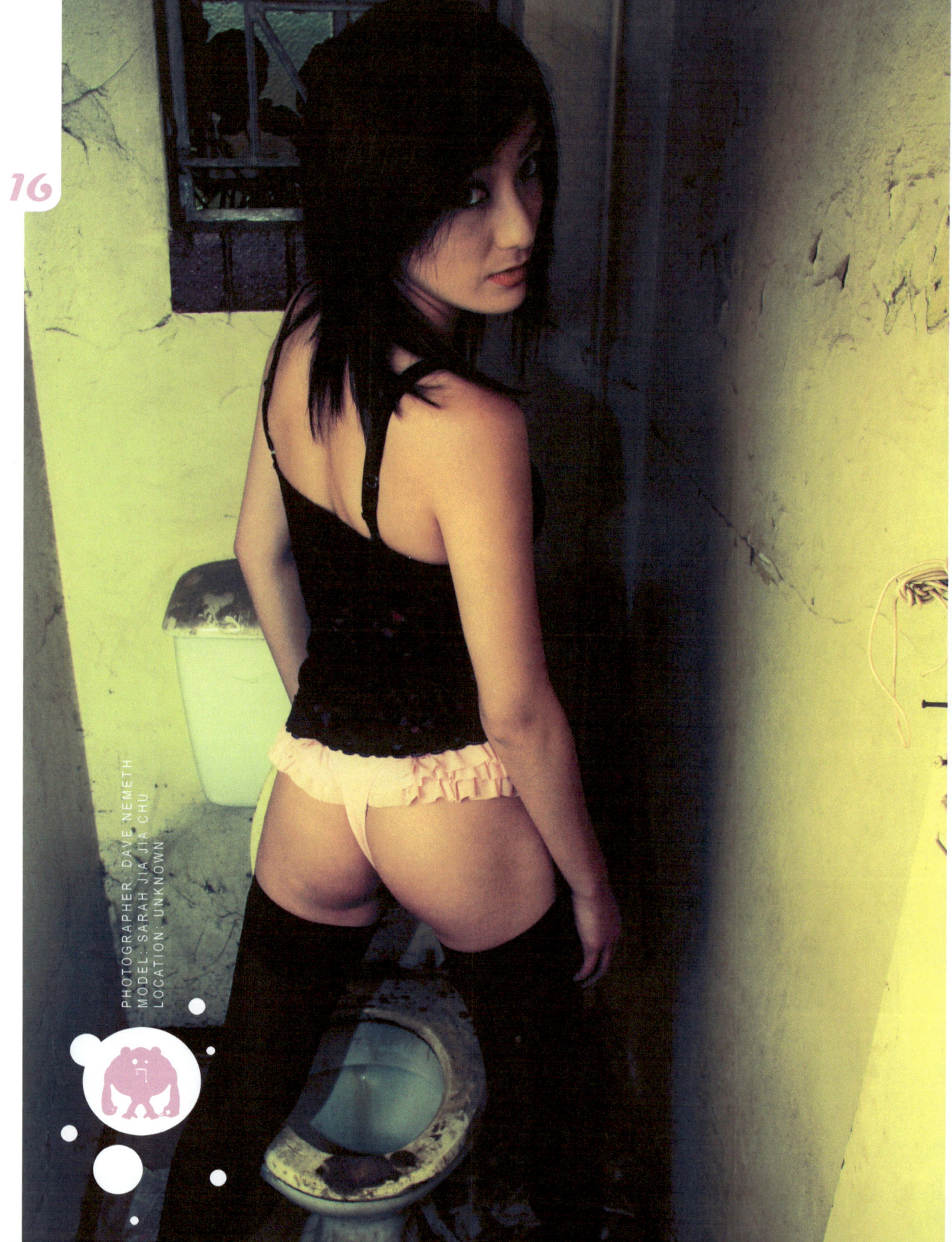

16

PHOTOGRAPHER: DAVE NEMETH
MODEL: SARAH JIA JIA CHU
LOCATION: UNKNOWN

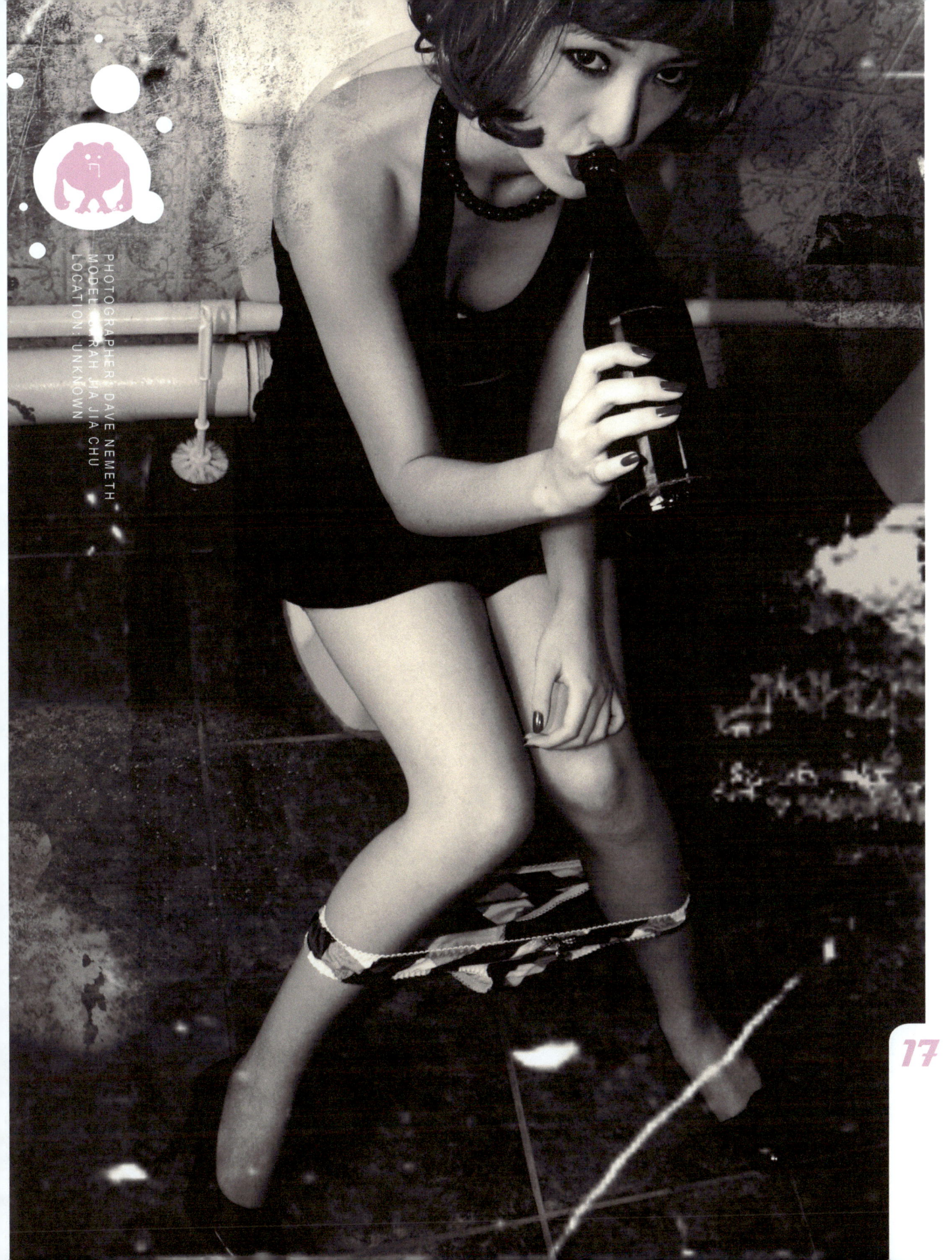

PHOTOGRAPHER: DAVE NEMETH
MODEL: SARAH HA JIA CHU
LOCATION: UNKNOWN

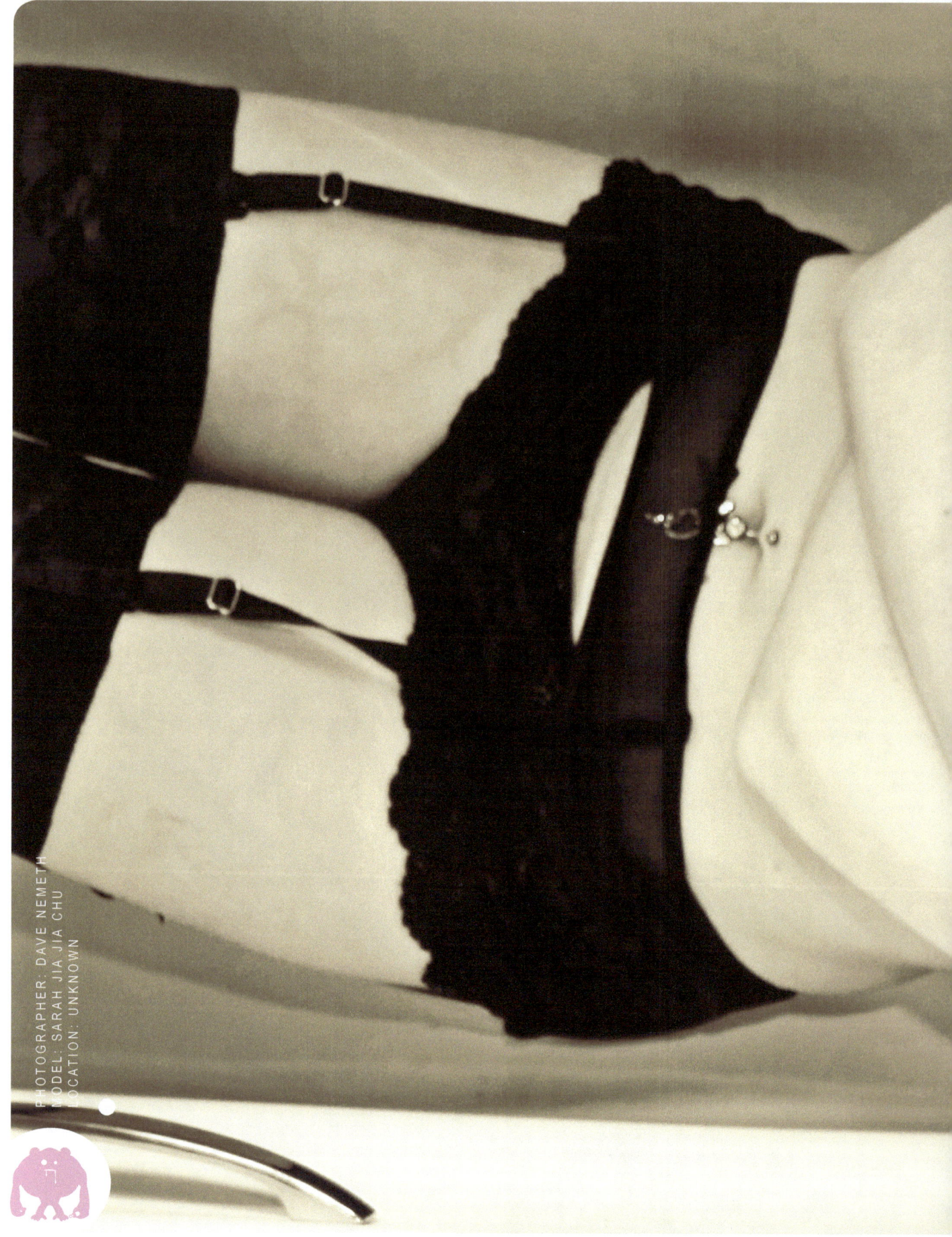

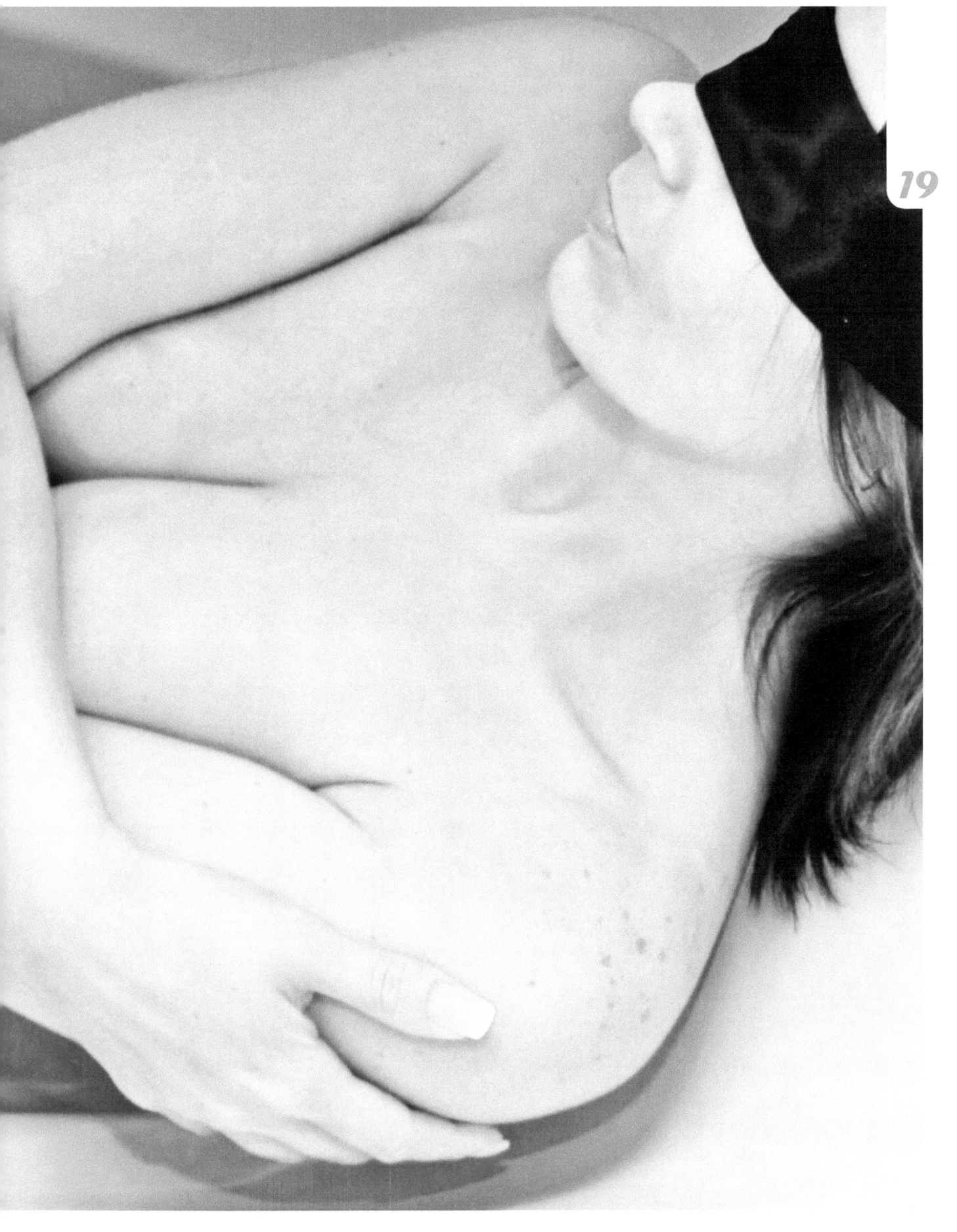

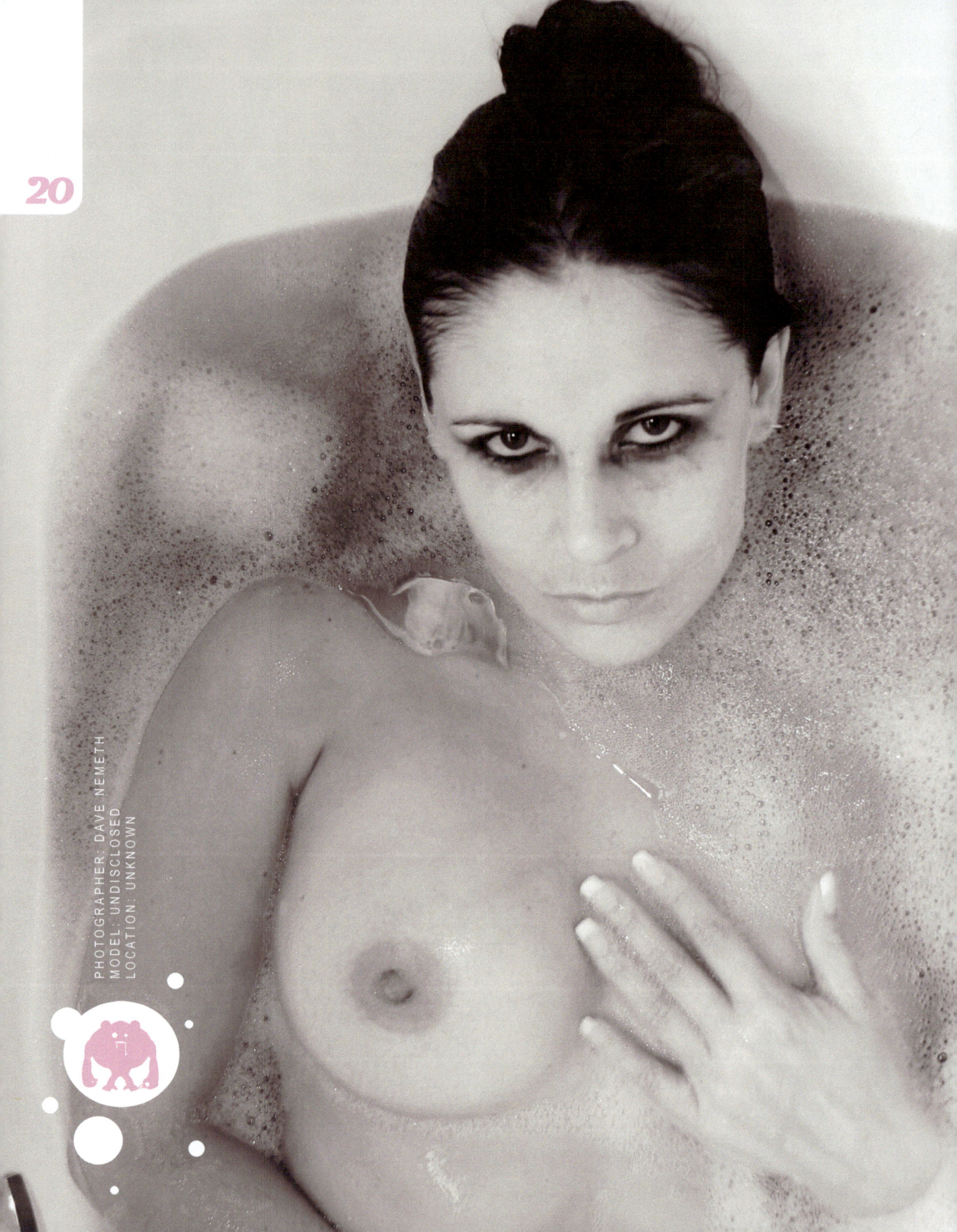

20

PHOTOGRAPHER: DAVE NEMETH
MODEL: UNDISCLOSED
LOCATION: UNKNOWN

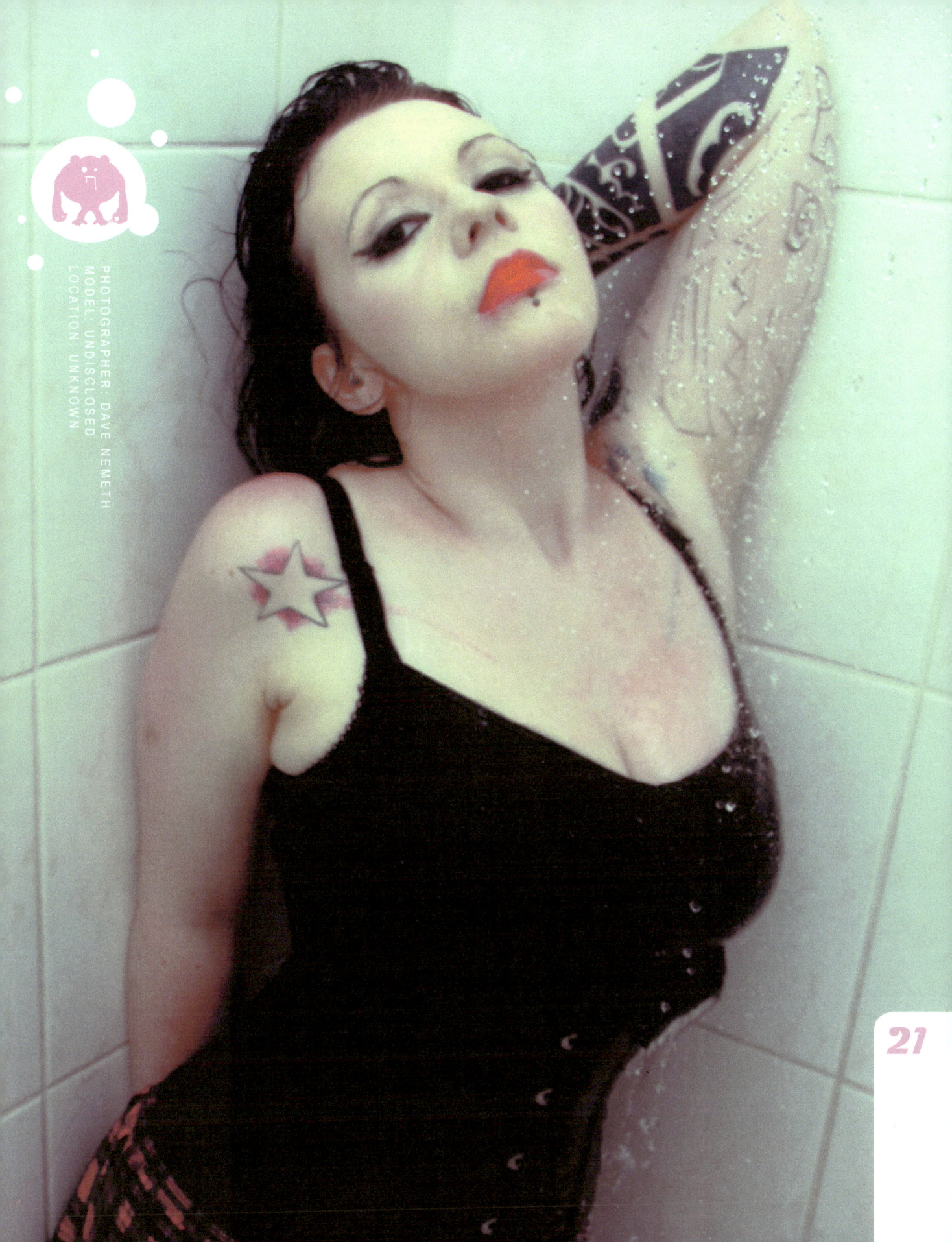

PHOTOGRAPHER: DAVE NEMETH
MODEL: UNDISCLOSED
LOCATION UNKNOWN

21

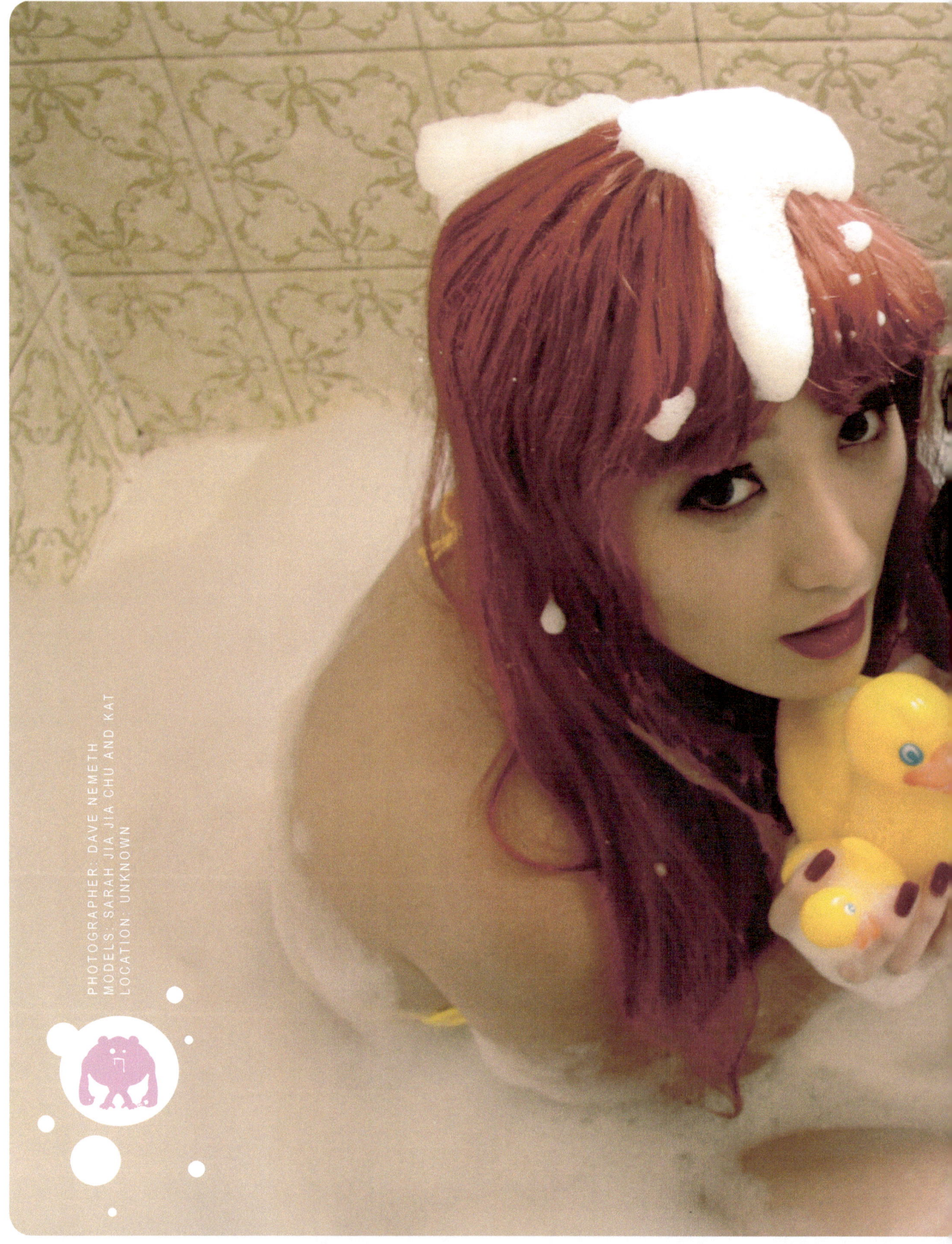

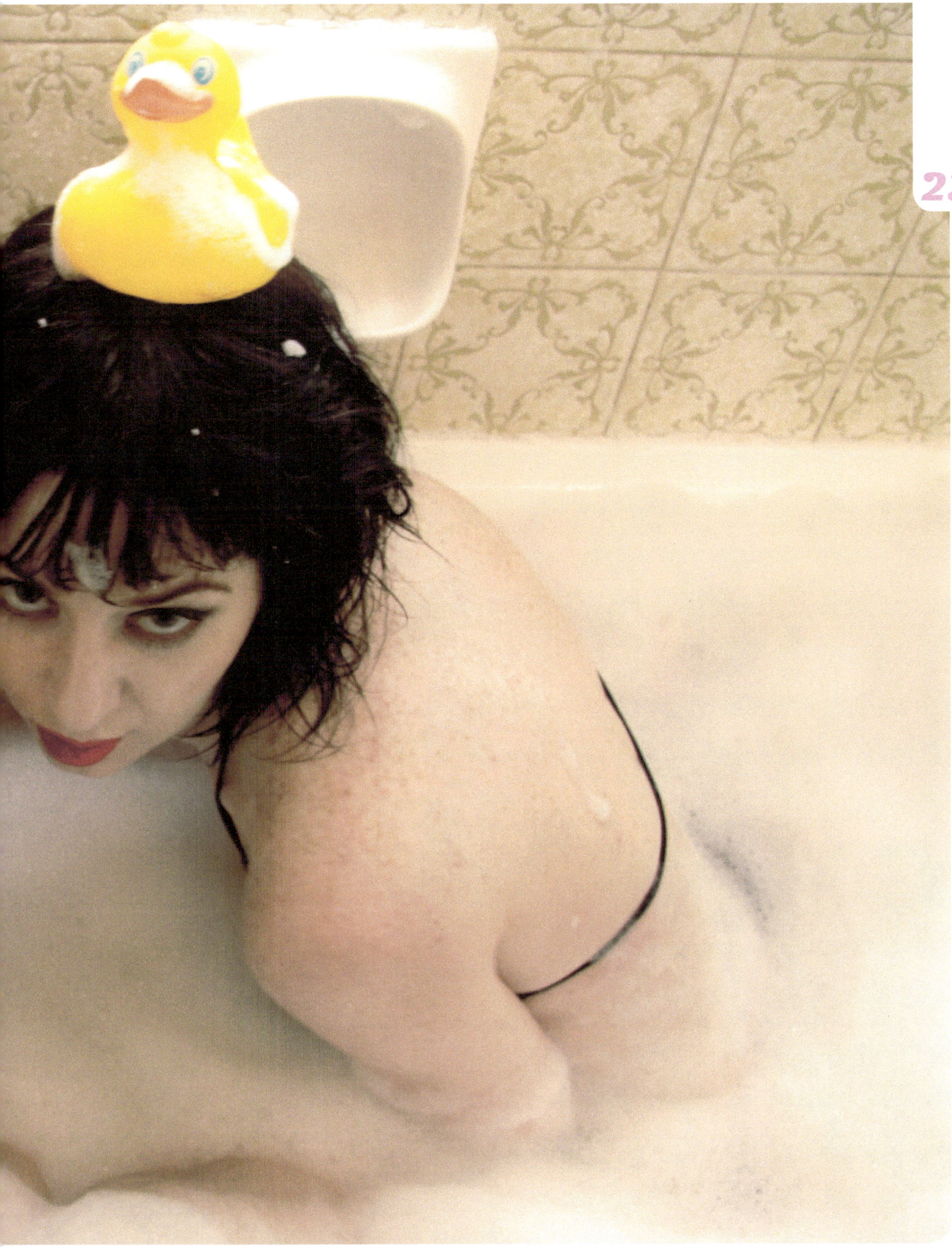

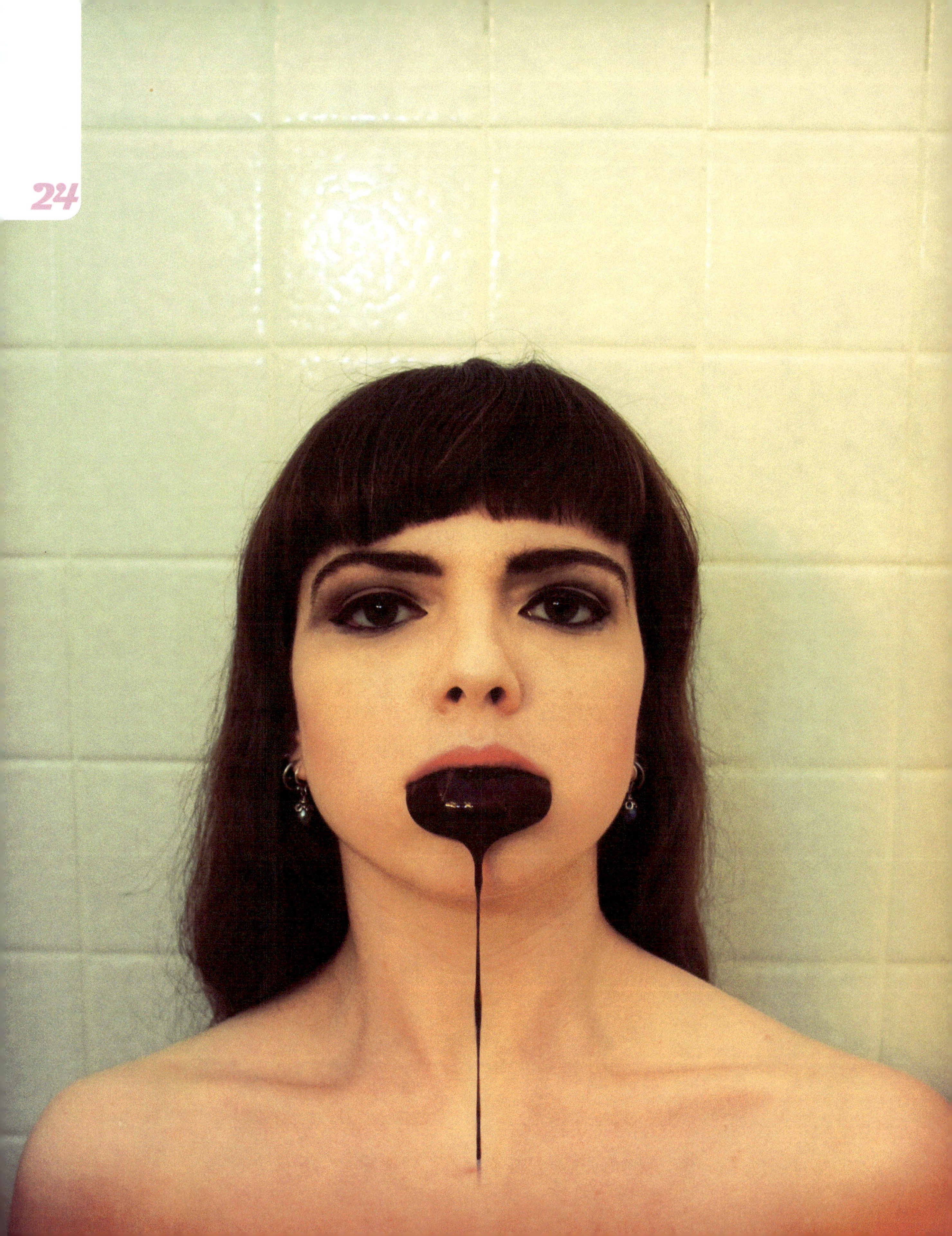

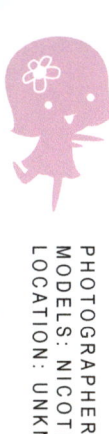

PHOTOGRAPHER: KAOS BEAUTY KLINIK
MODELS: NICOTINE
LOCATION: UNKNOWN (USA)

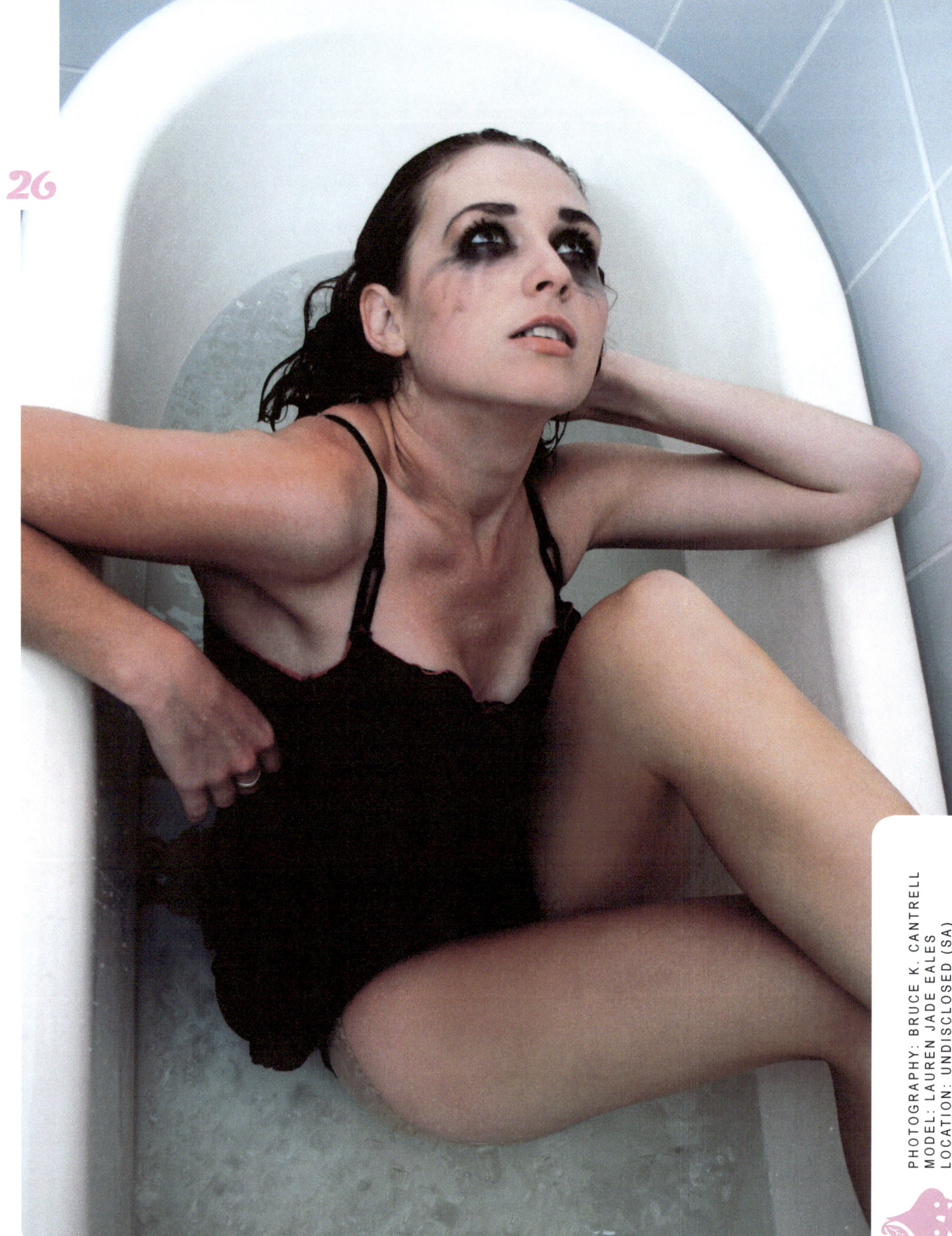

PHOTOGRAPHY: BRUCE K. CANTRELL
MODEL: LAUREN JADE EALES
LOCATION: UNDISCLOSED (SA)

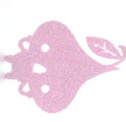

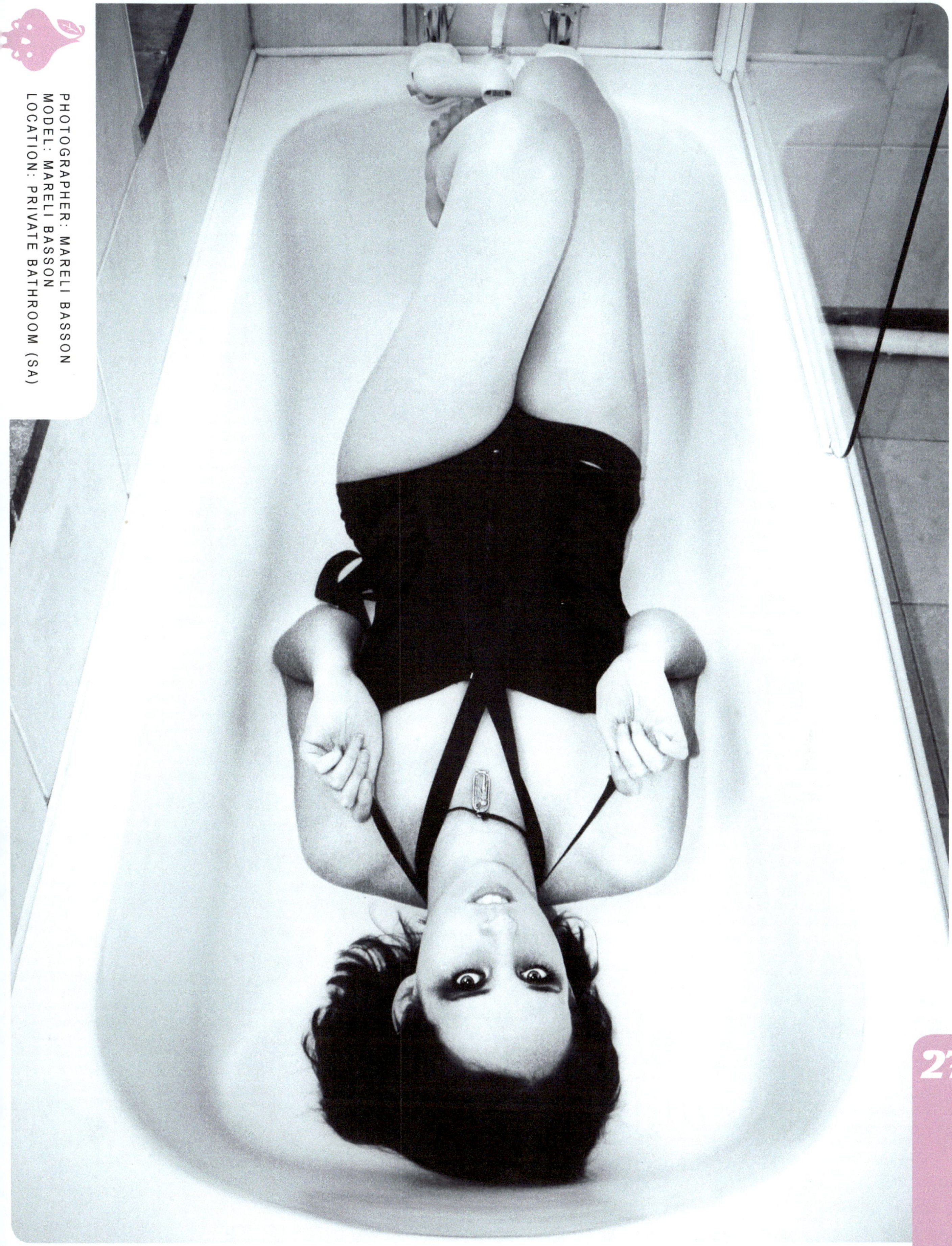

PHOTOGRAPHER: MARELI BASSON
MODEL: MARELI BASSON
LOCATION: PRIVATE BATHROOM (SA)

27

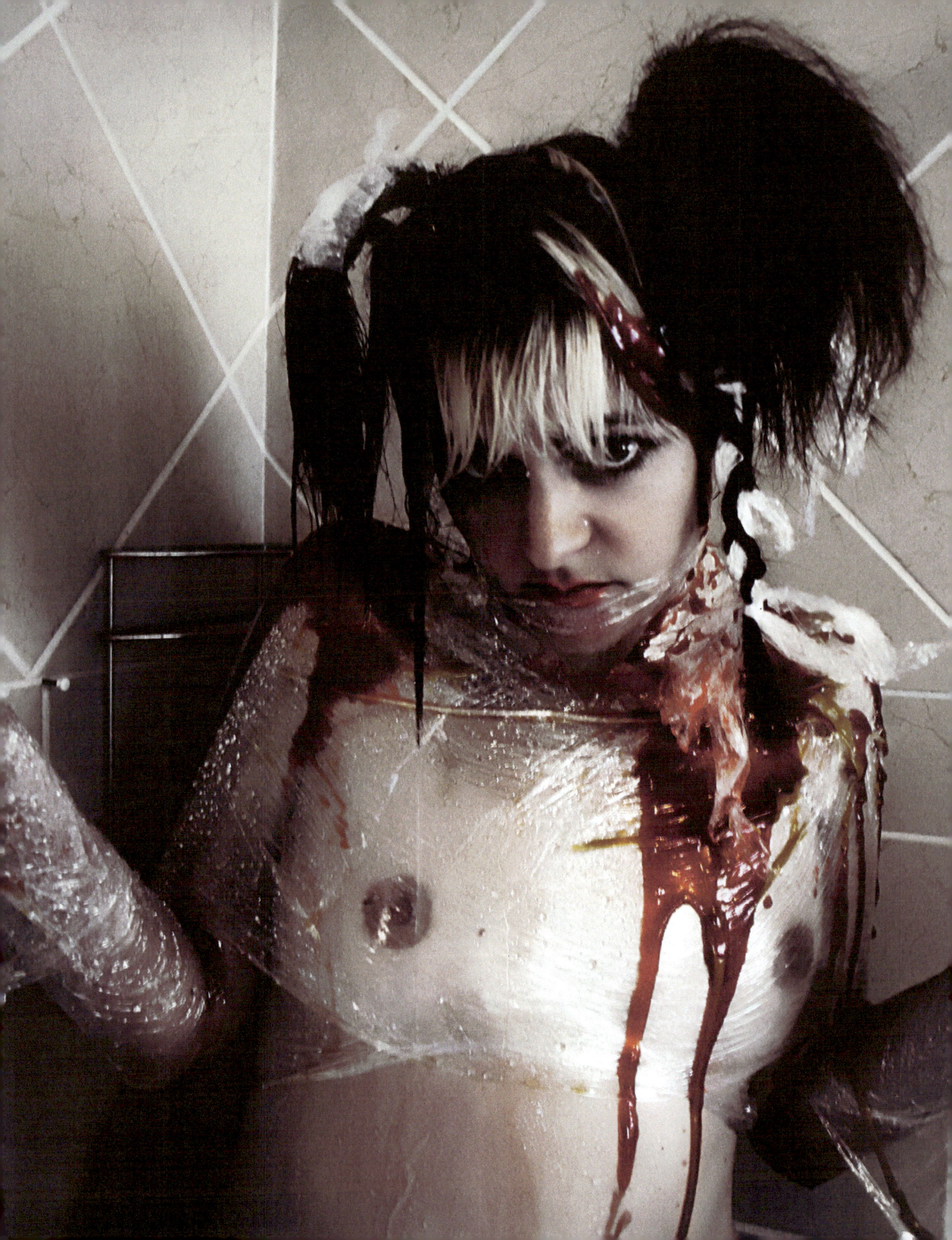

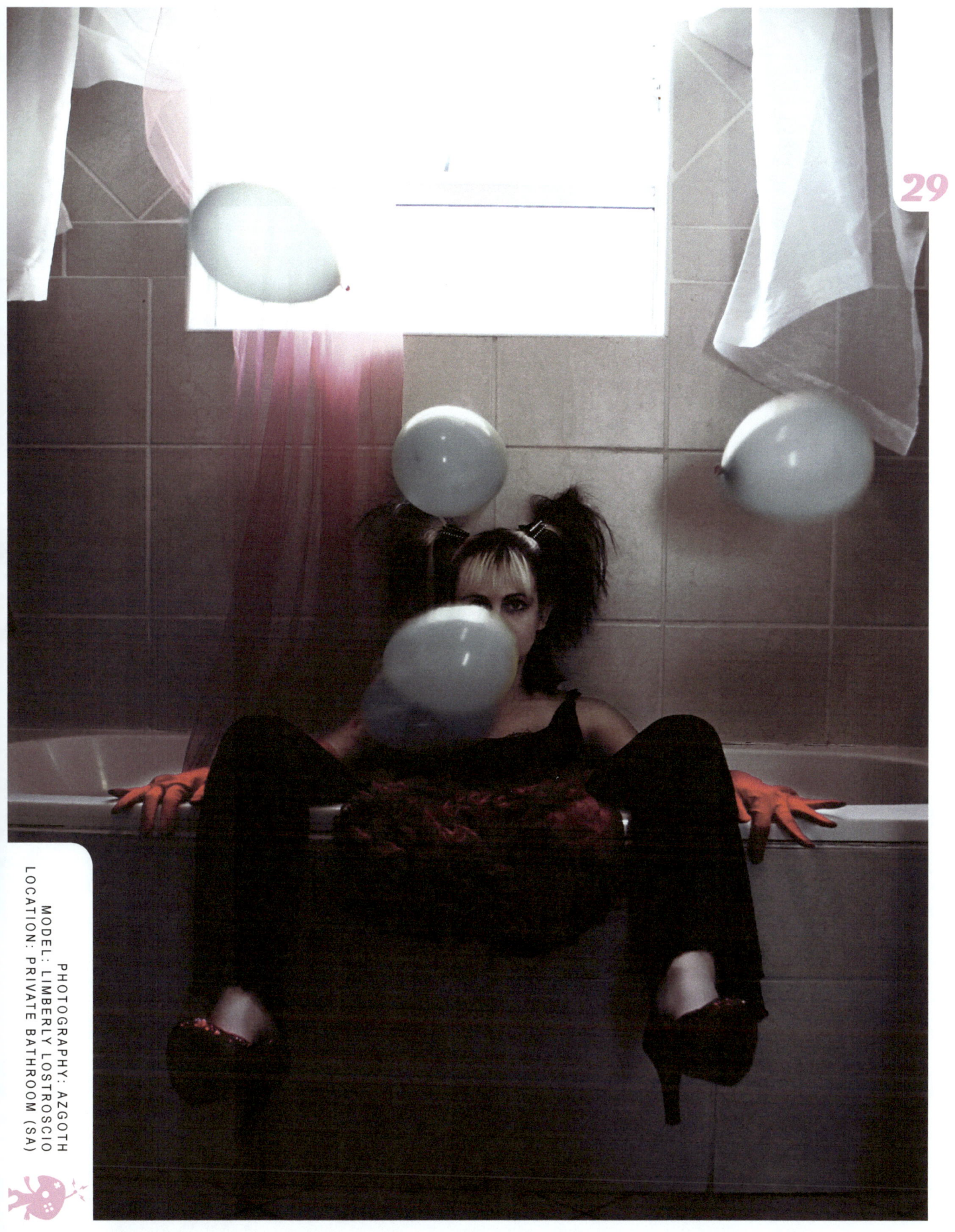

PHOTOGRAPHY: AZGOTH
MODEL: LIMBERLY LOSTROSCIO
LOCATION: PRIVATE BATHROOM (SA)

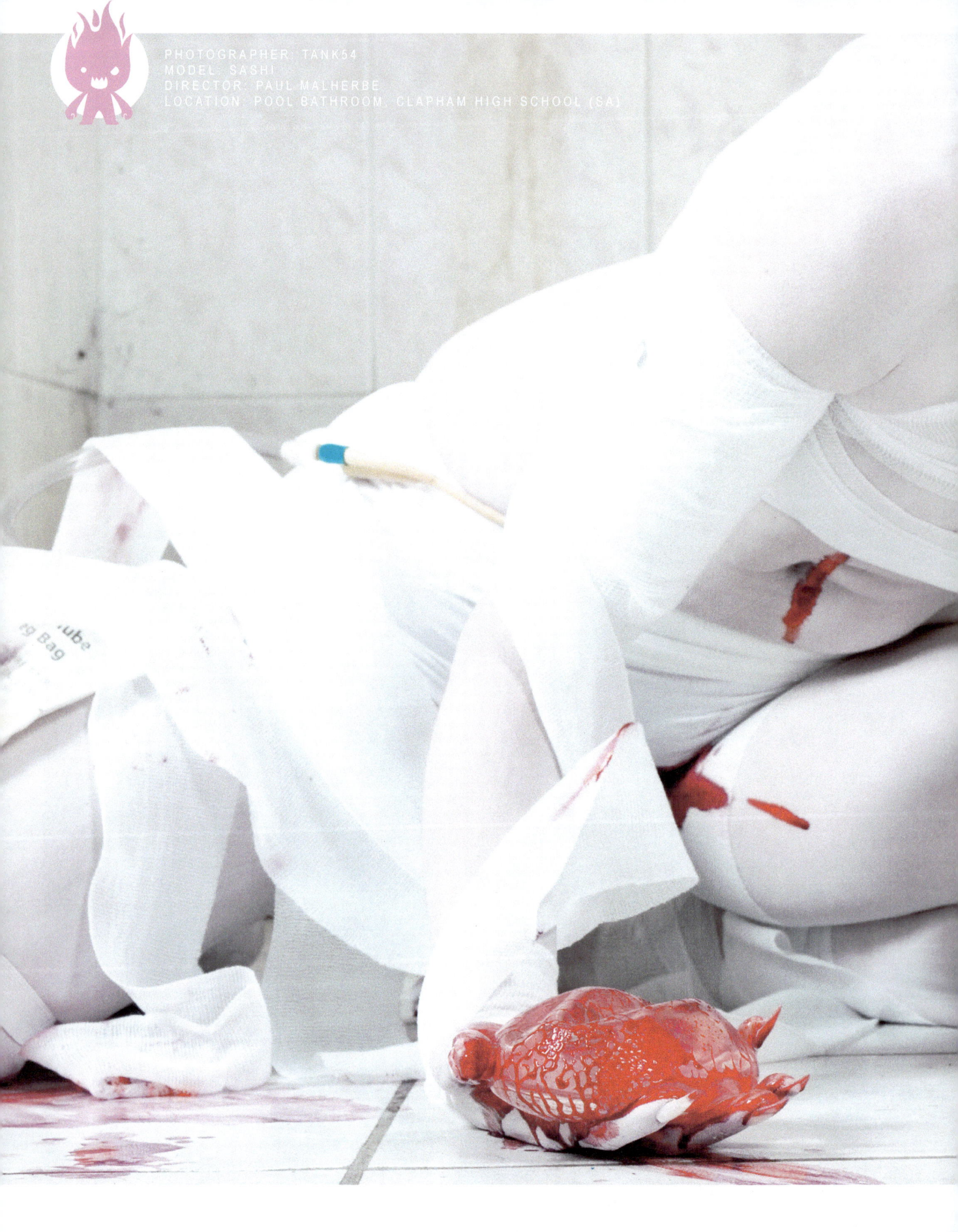

PHOTOGRAPHER: TANK54
MODEL: SASHI
DIRECTOR: PAUL MALHERBE
LOCATION: POOL BATHROOM, CLAPHAM HIGH SCHOOL (SA)

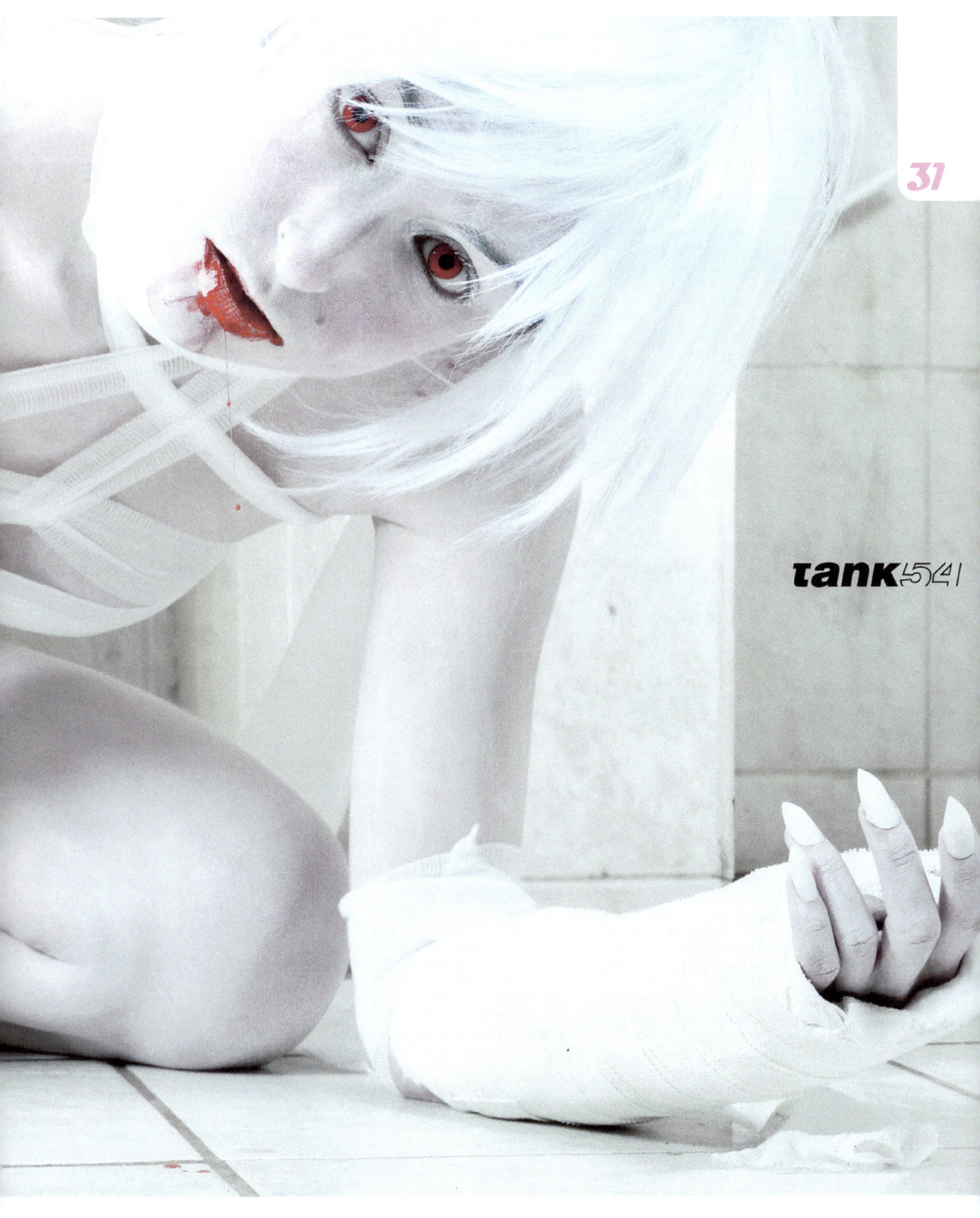

tank 54

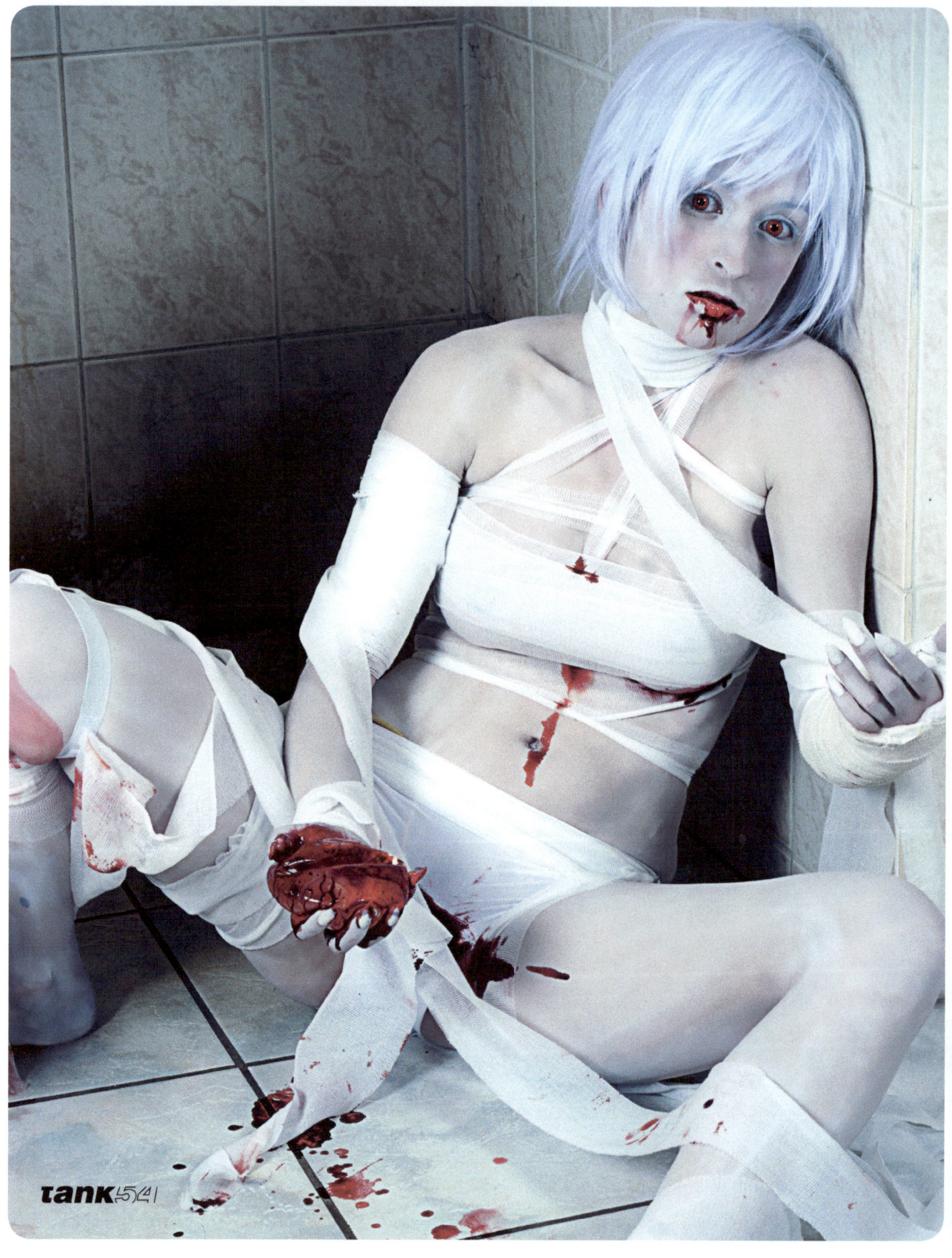

tank54

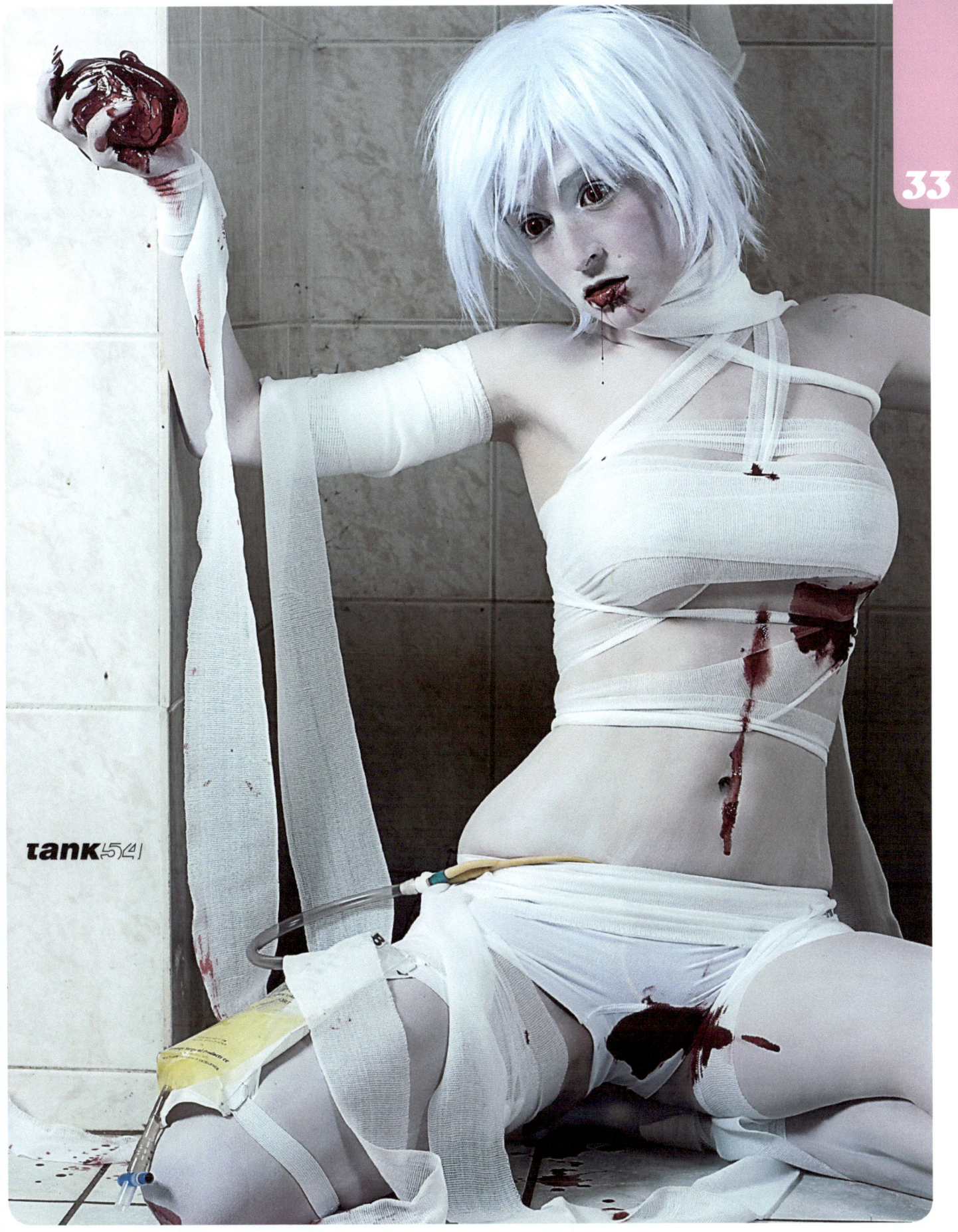

tank54

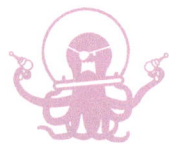

PHOTOGRAPHY: ZELDA WELGEMOED AKA WICKEDEE
MODEL: ALTA LOUW
LOCATION: NORTHCLIFF, JHB (SA)

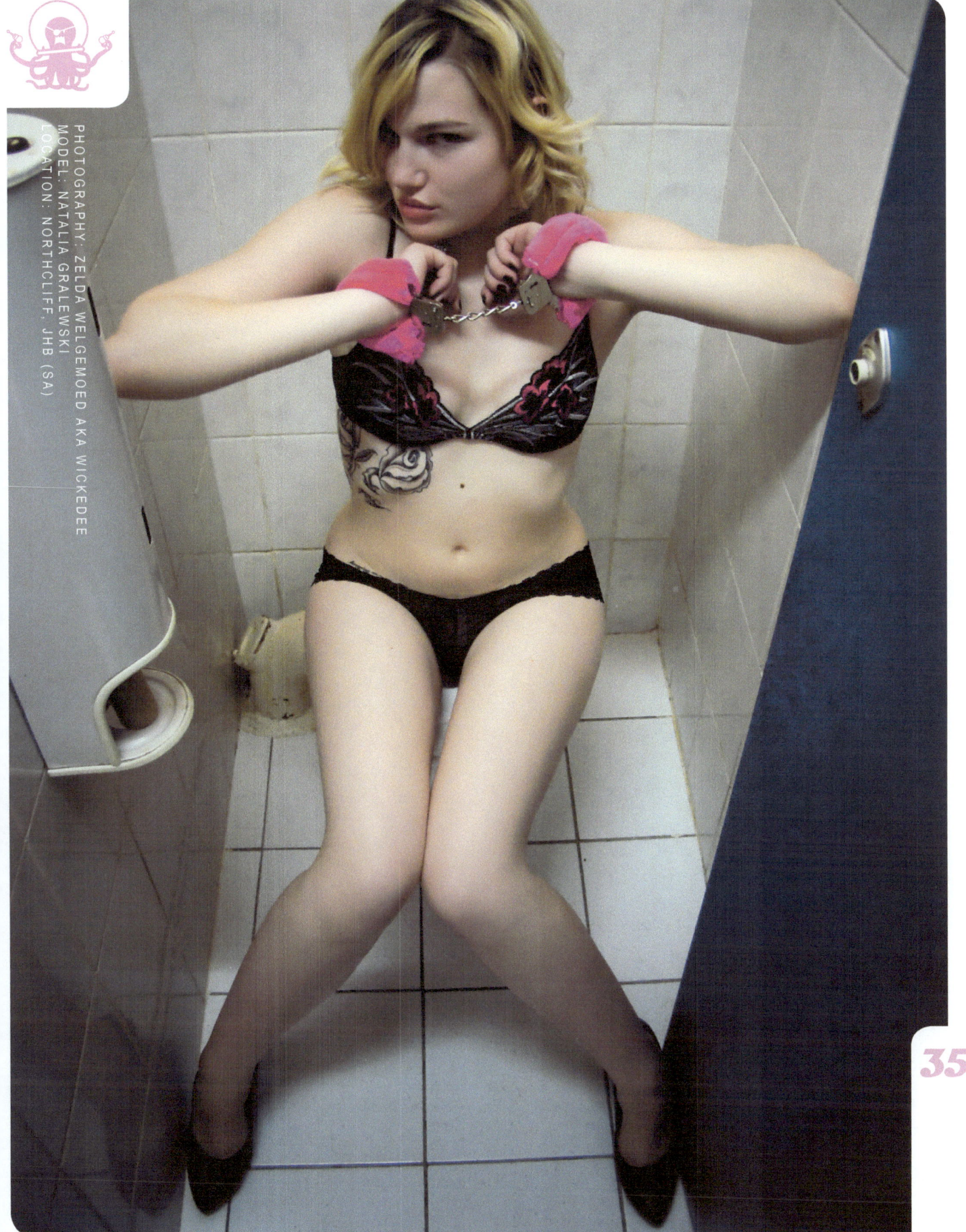

PHOTOGRAPHY: ZELDA WELGEMOED AKA WICKEDEE
MODEL: NATALIA GRALEWSKI
LOCATION: NORTHCLIFF, JHB (SA)

35

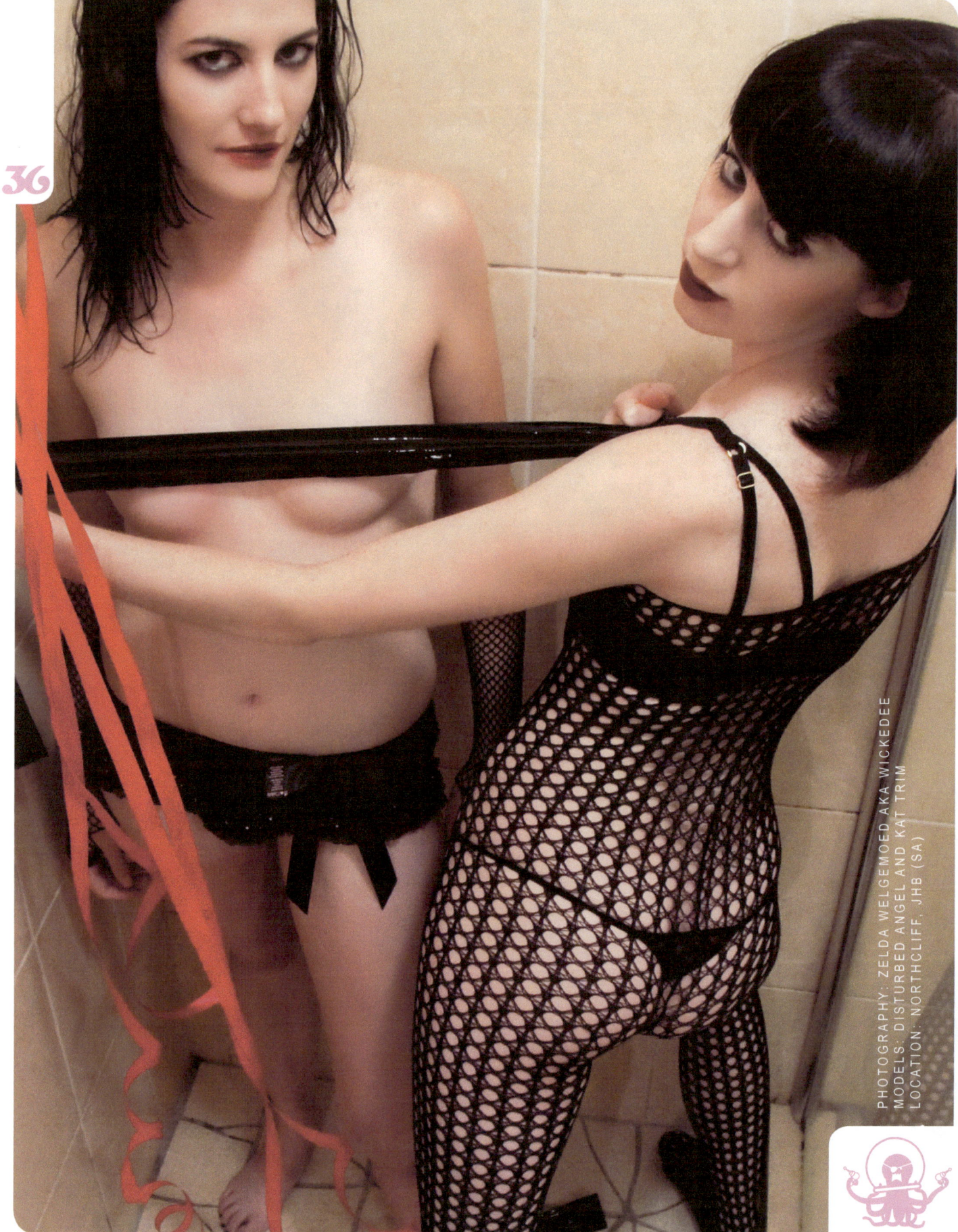

PHOTOGRAPHY: ZELDA WELGEMOED AKA WICKEDEE
MODELS: DISTURBED ANGEL AND KAT TRIM
LOCATION: NORTHCLIFF, JHB (SA)

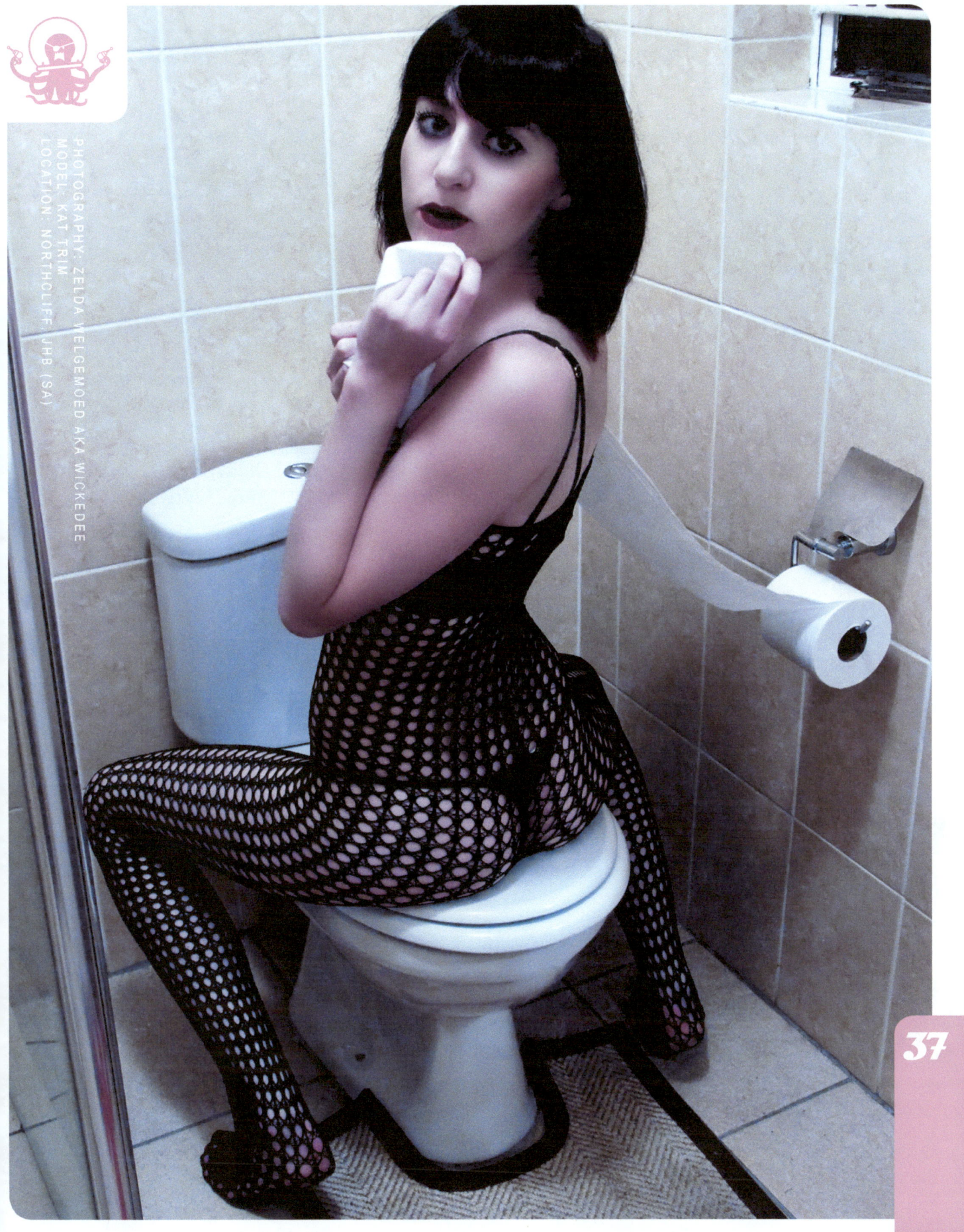

PHOTOGRAPHY: ZELDA WELGEMOED AKA WICKEDEE
MODEL: KAT TRIM
LOCATION: NORTHCLIFF JHB (SA)

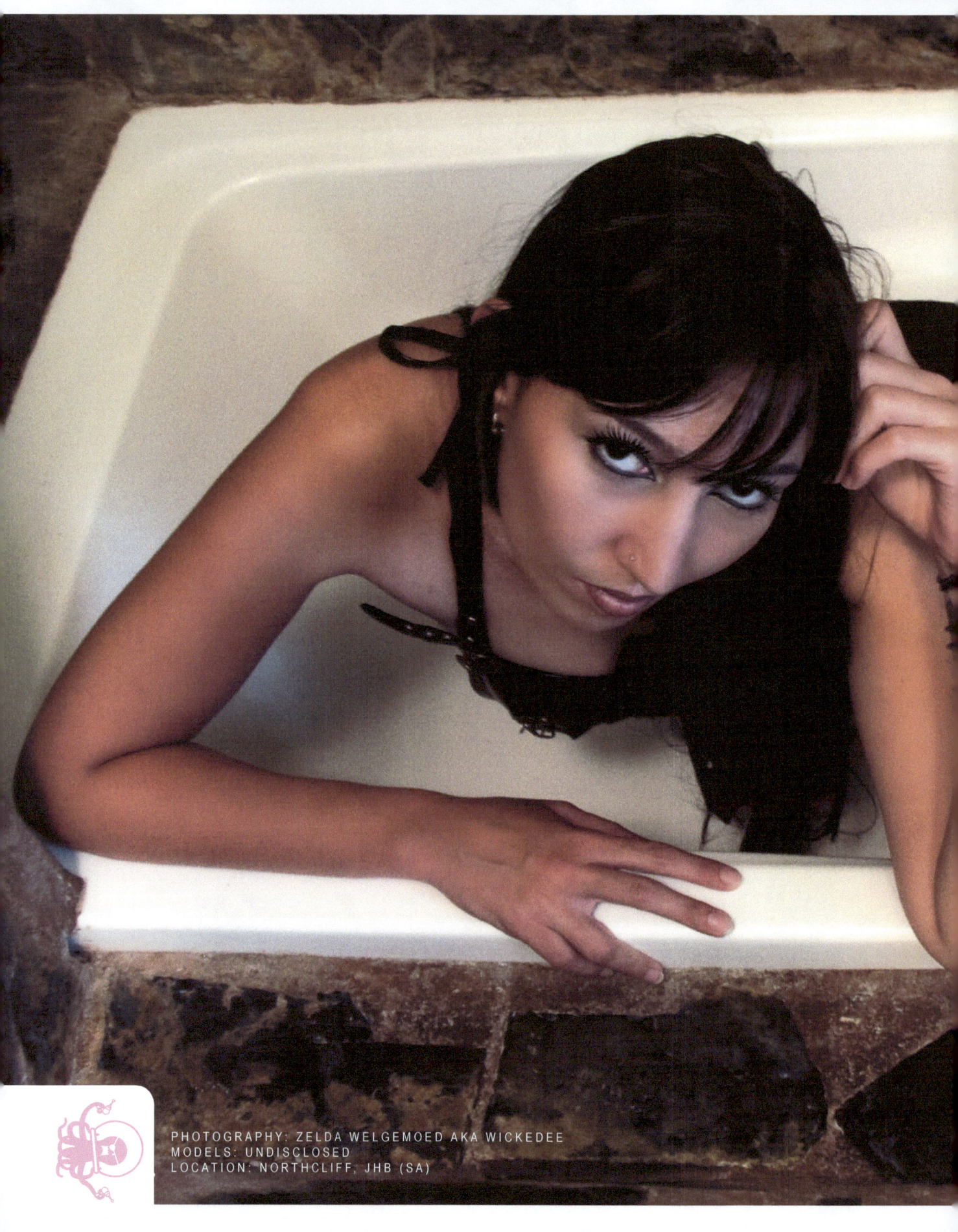

PHOTOGRAPHY: ZELDA WELGEMOED AKA WICKEDEE
MODELS: UNDISCLOSED
LOCATION: NORTHCLIFF, JHB (SA)

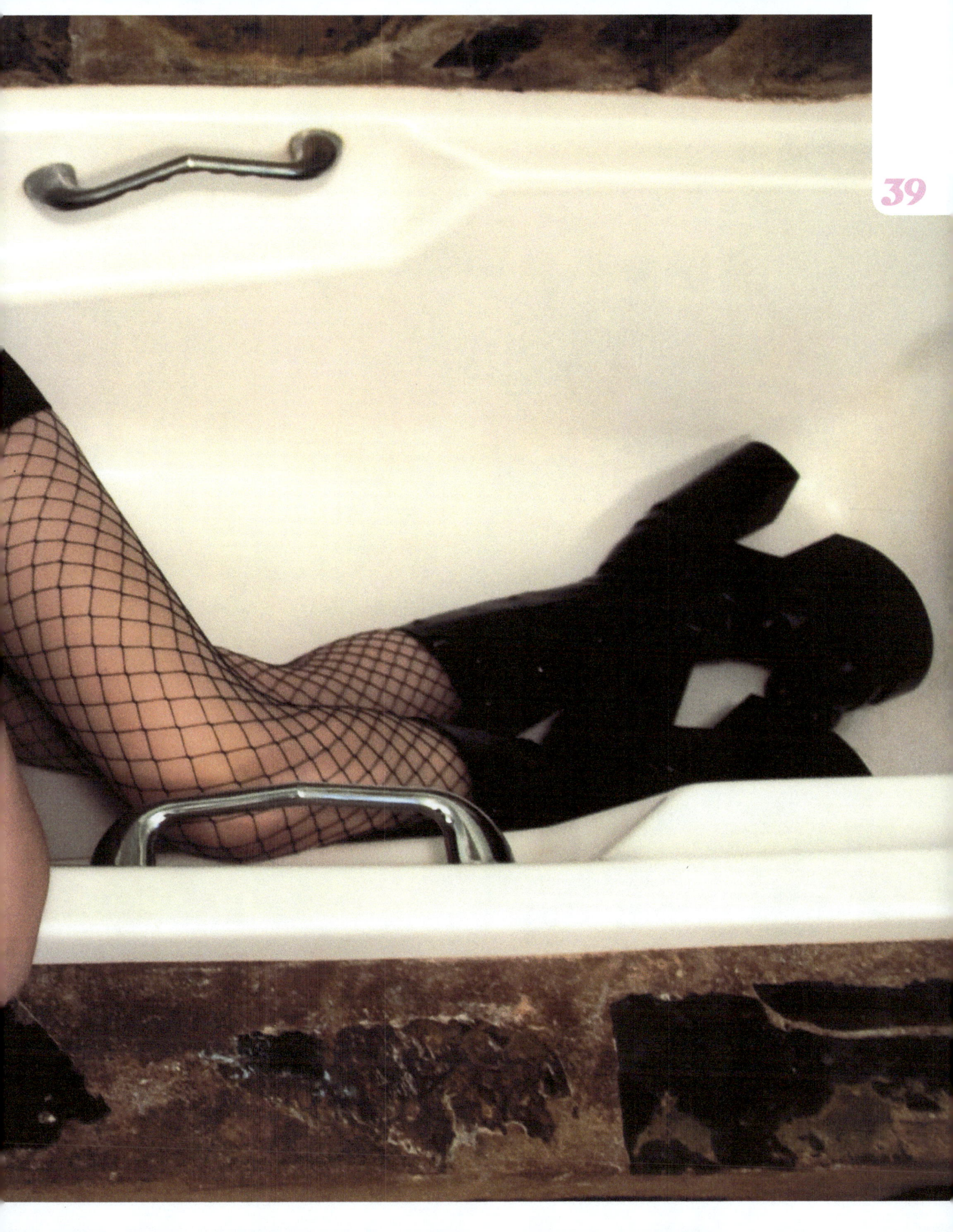

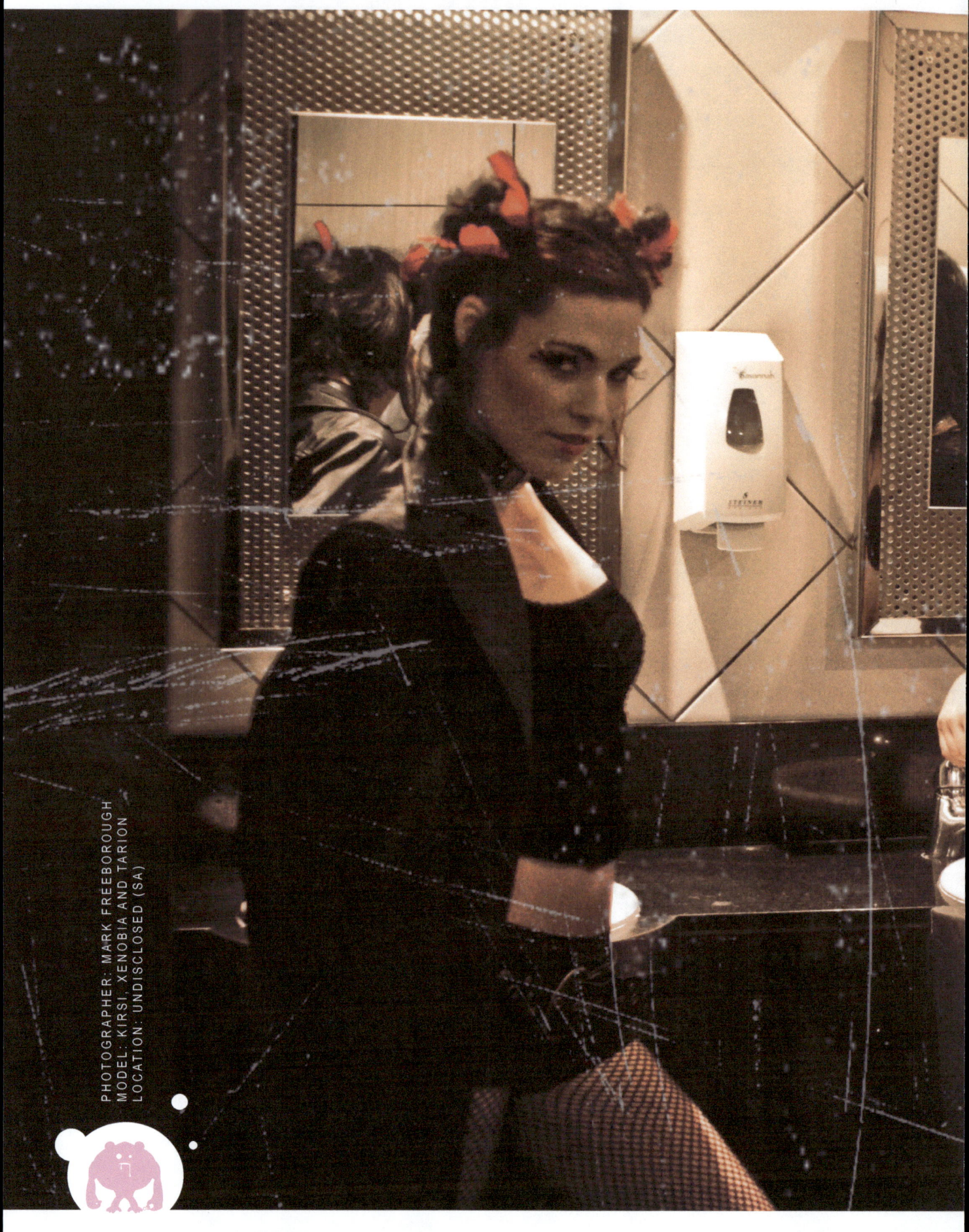

PHOTOGRAPHER: MARK FREEBOROUGH
MODEL: KIRSI, XENOBIA AND TARION
LOCATION: UNDISCLOSED (SA)

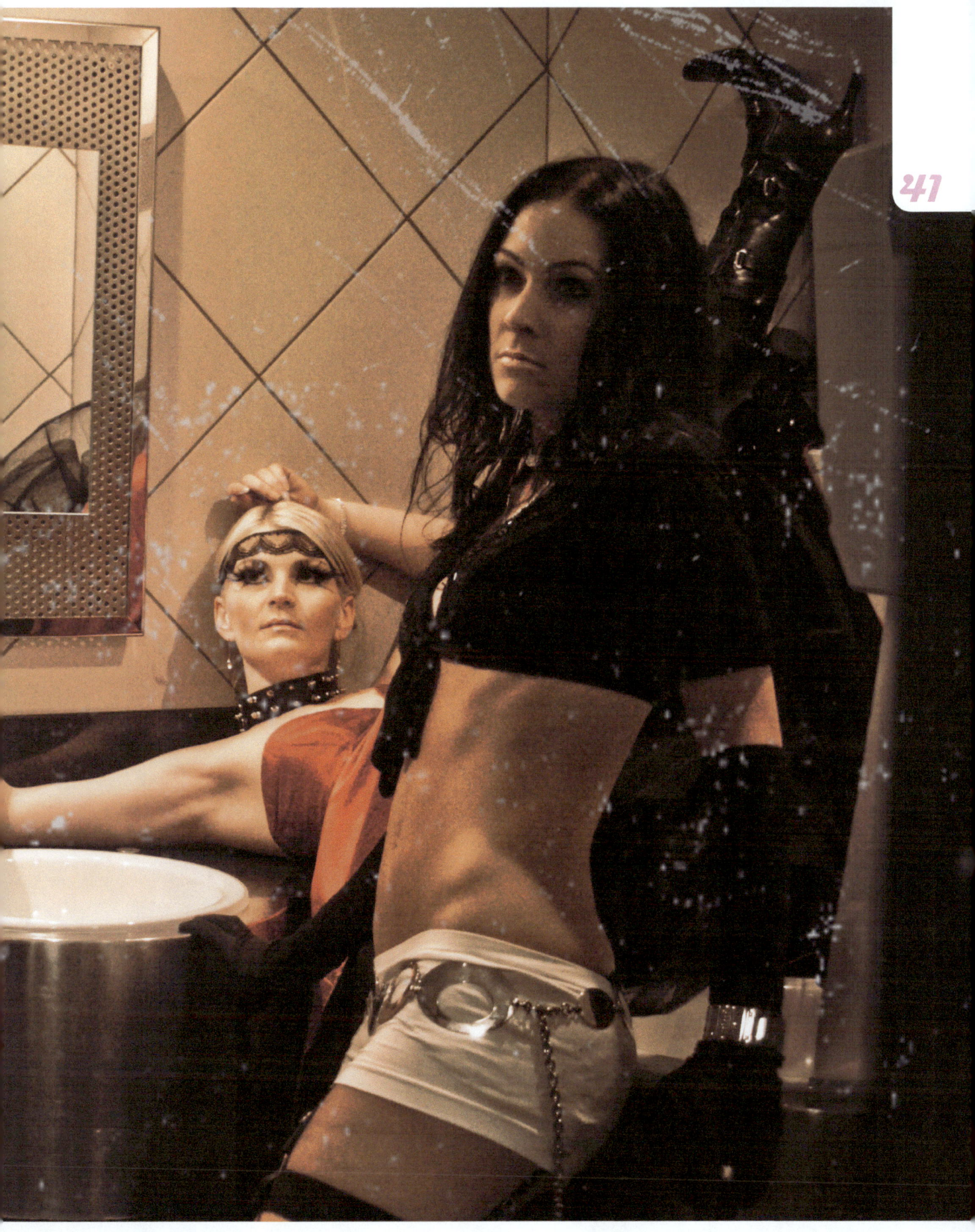

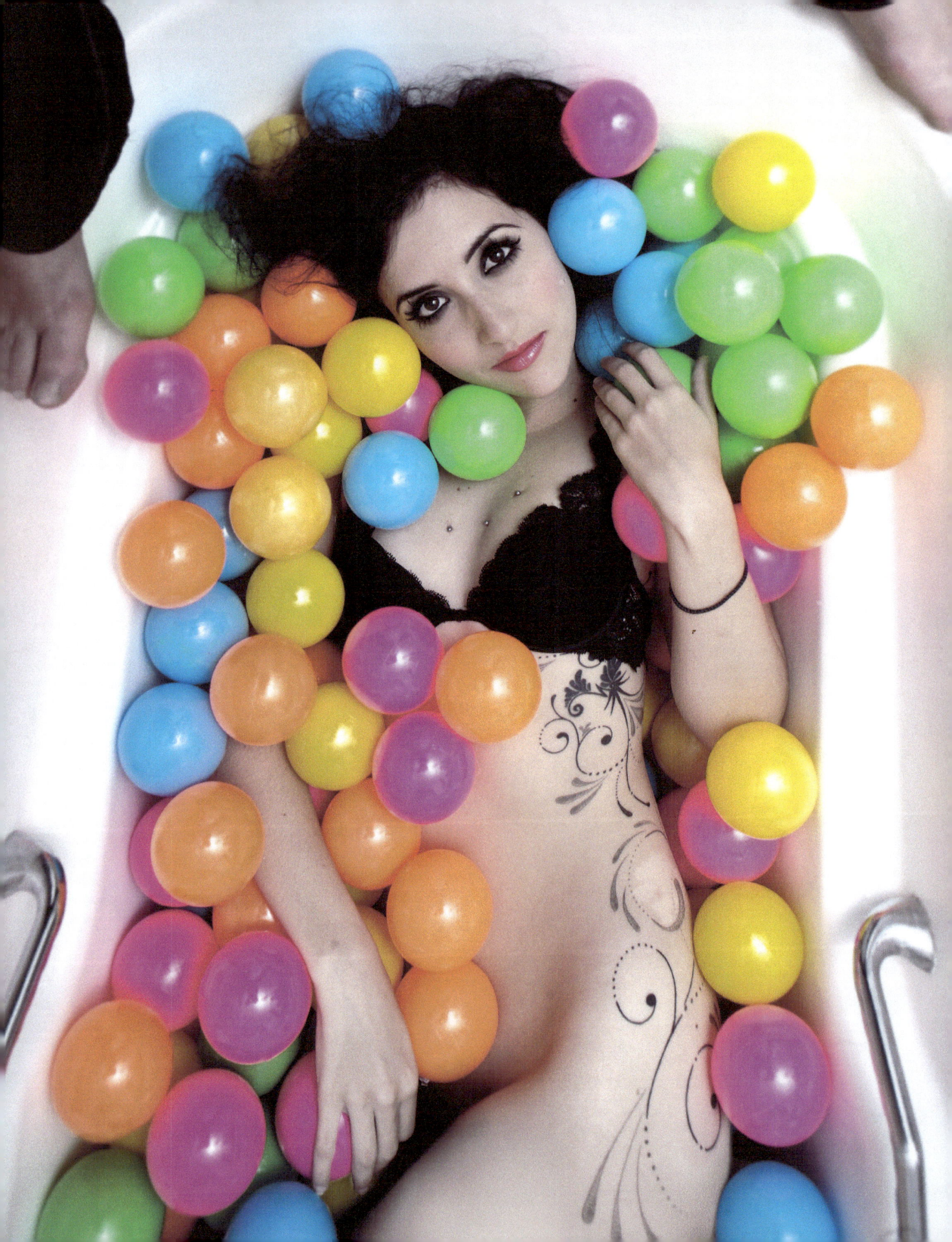

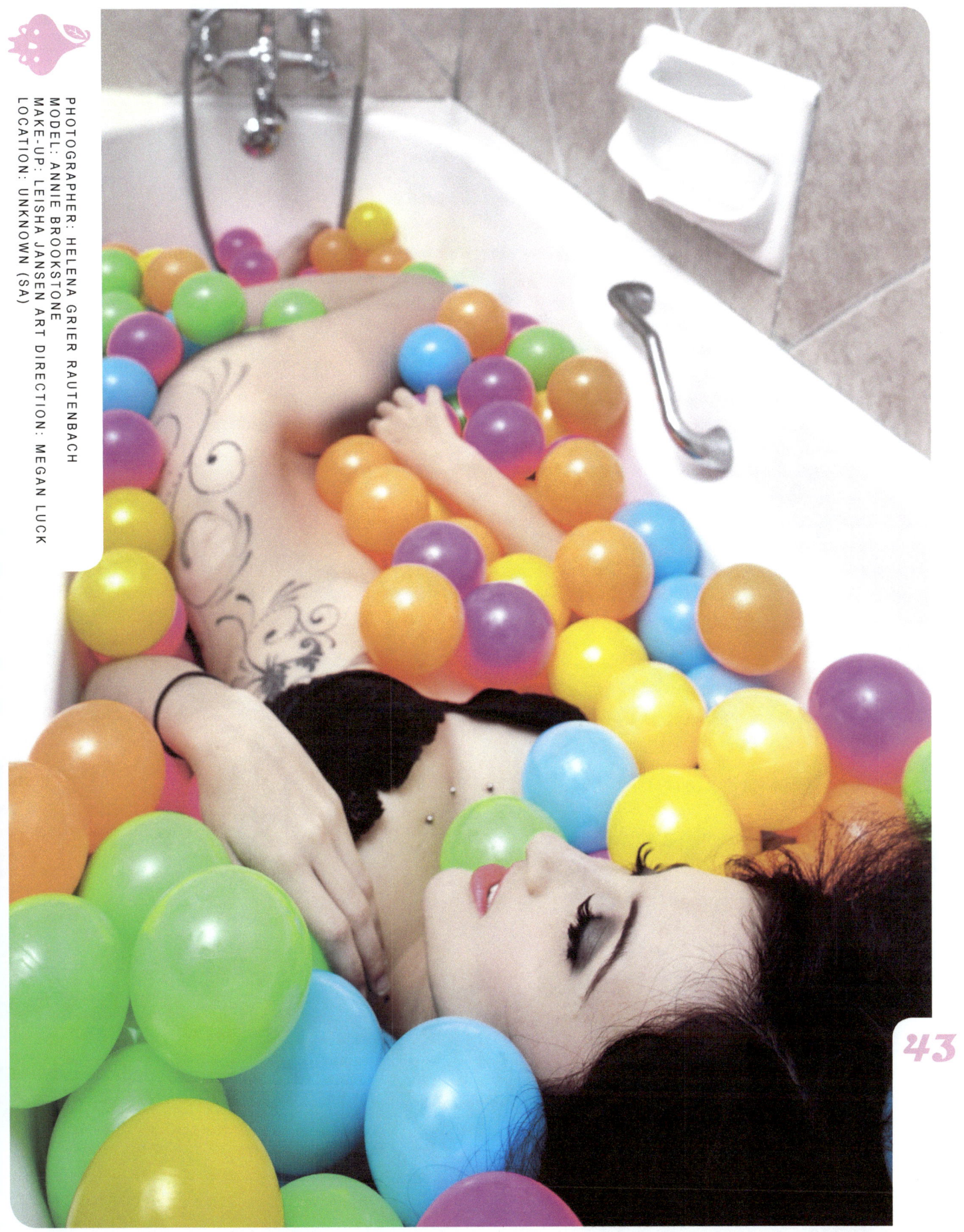

PHOTOGRAPHER: HELENA GRIER RAUTENBACH
MODEL: ANNIE BROOKSTONE
MAKE-UP: LEISHA JANSEN ART DIRECTION: MEGAN LUCK
LOCATION: UNKNOWN (SA)

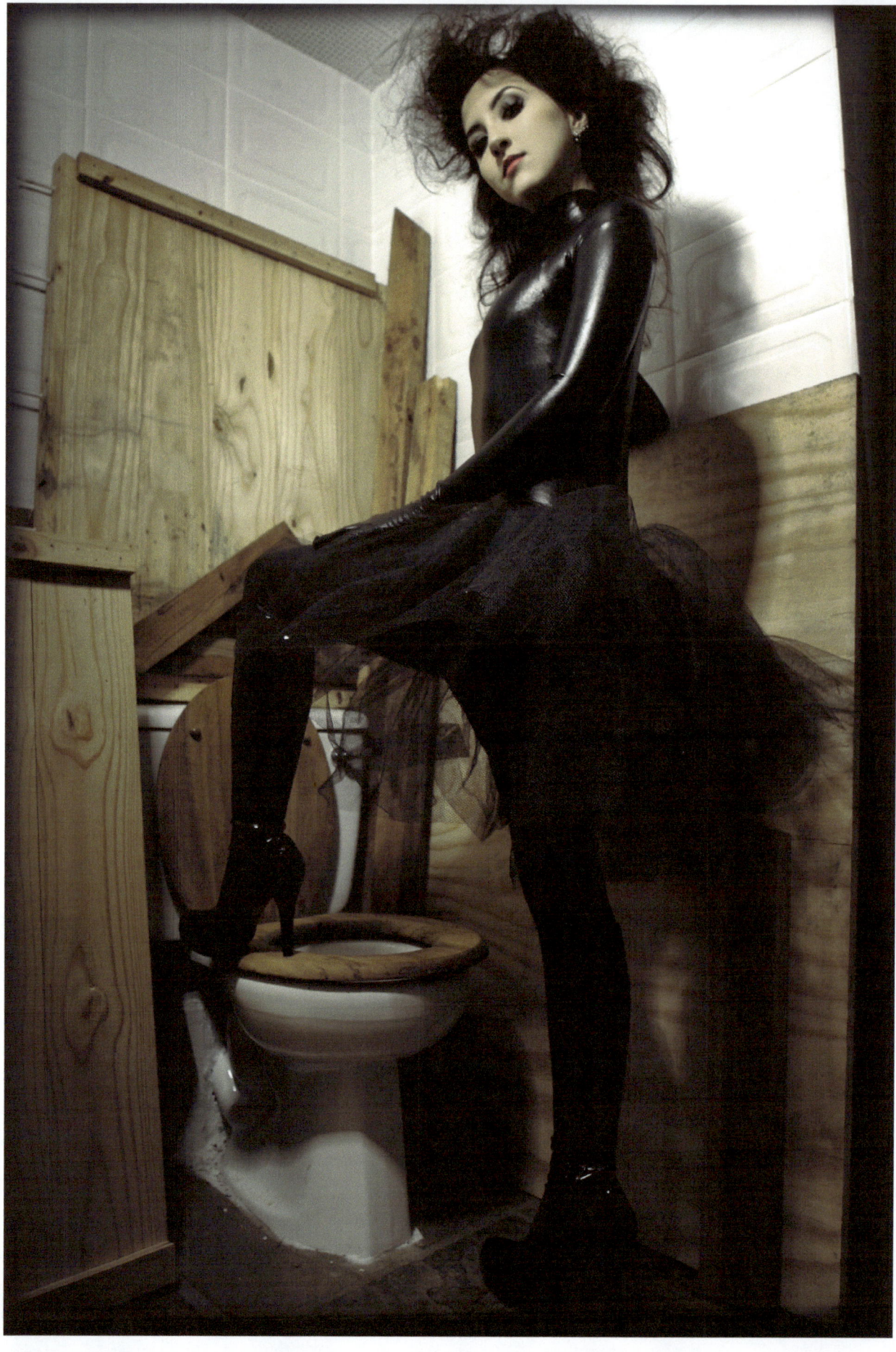

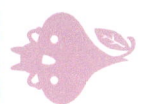

PHOTOGRAPHER: HELENA GRIER RAUTENBACH
MODEL: ANNIE BROOKSTONE
MAKE-UP: LEISHA JANSEN ART DIRECTION: MEGAN LUCK
LOCATION: UNKNOWN (SA)

45

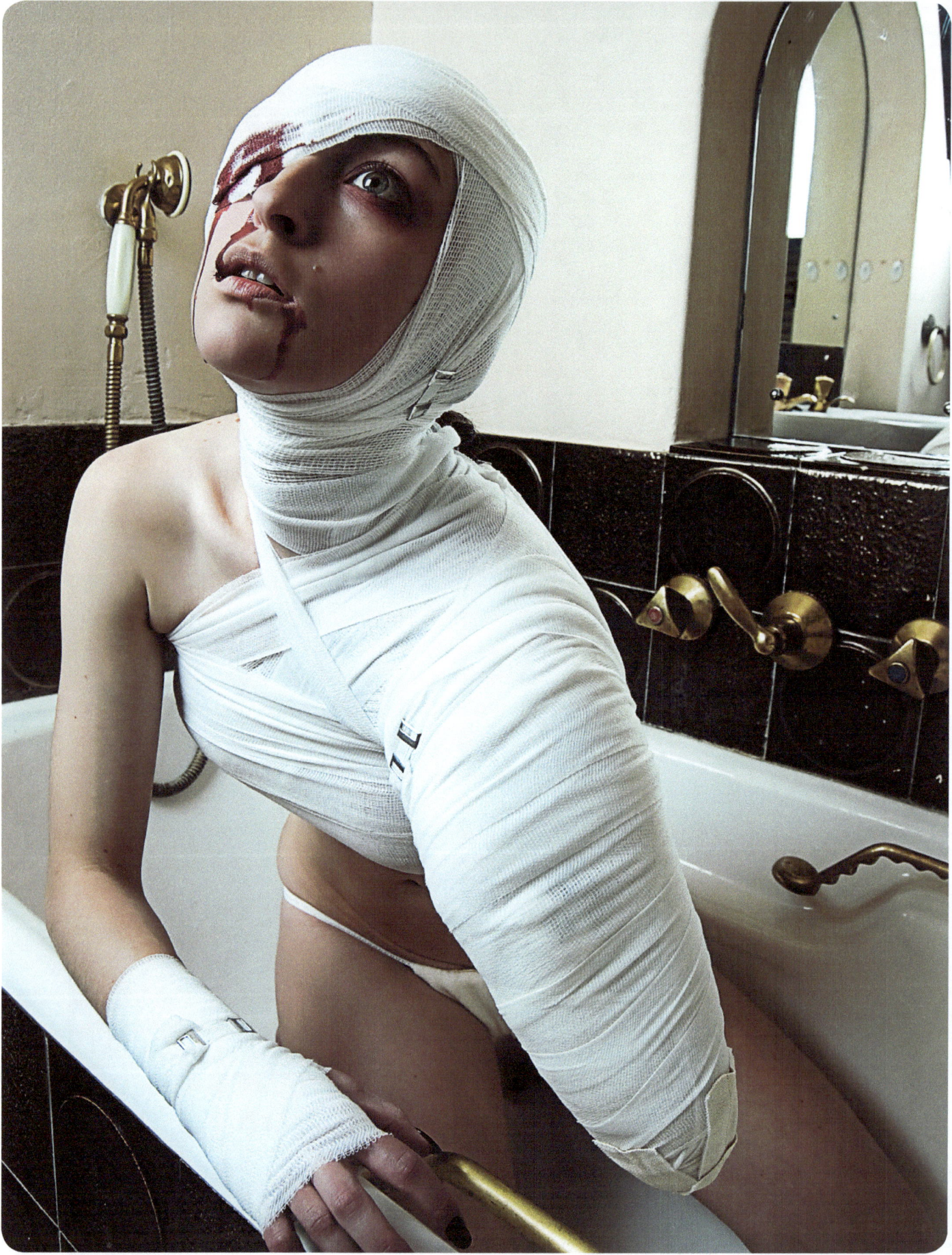

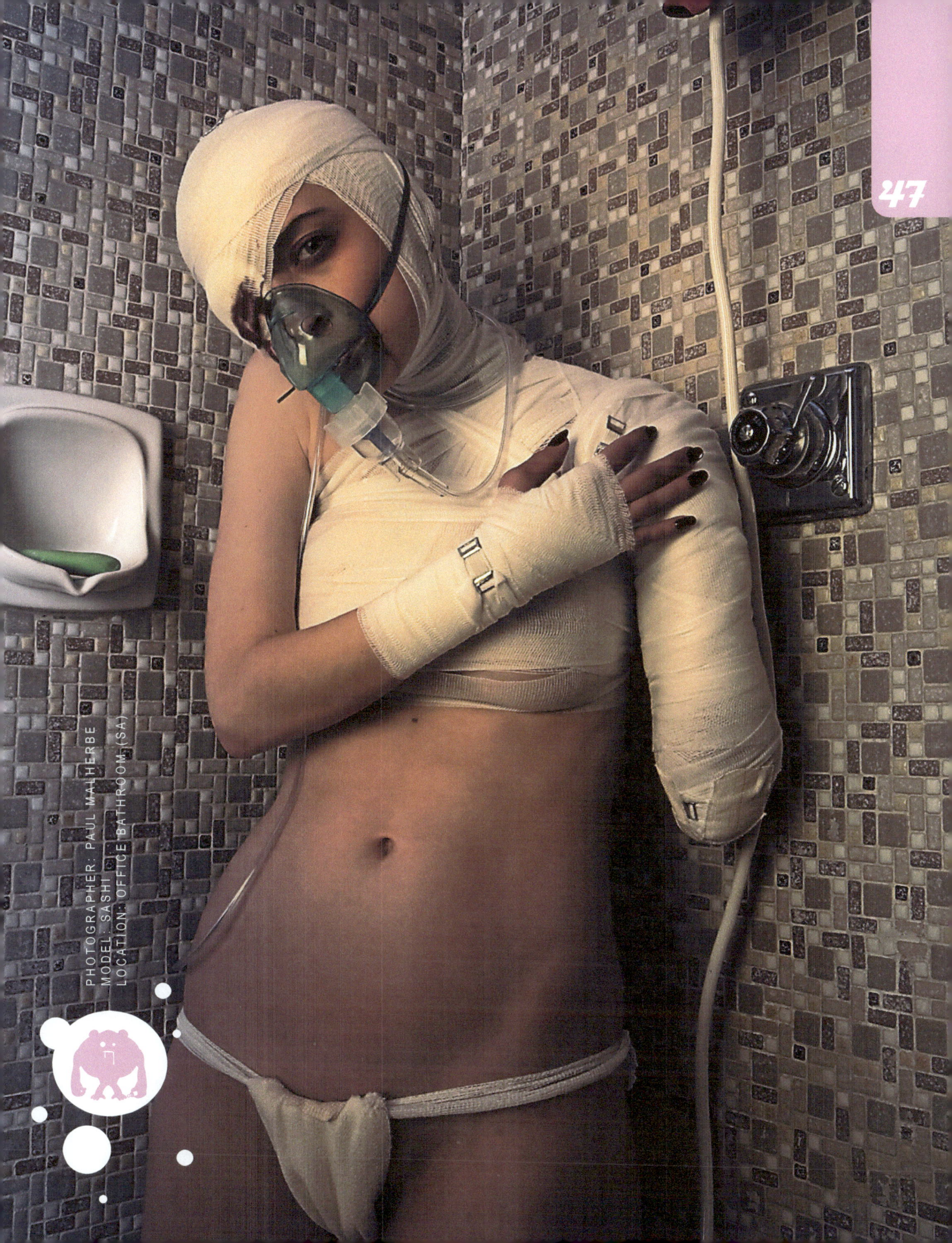

PHOTOGRAPHER: PAUL MALHERBE
MODEL: SASHI
LOCATION: OFFICE BATHROOM (SA)

Powder Room

a sumo studios publication

PHOTOGRAPHER:PAUL MALHERBE
MODEL: SASHI